The New York Times

CHANGING PERSPECTIVES

Religious Freedom

THE NEW YORK TIMES EDITORIAL STAFF

Published in 2020 by New York Times Educational Publishing
in association with The Rosen Publishing Group, Inc.
29 East 21st Street, New York, NY 10010

First Edition

The New York Times
Alex Ward: Editorial Director, Book Development
Phyllis Collazo: Photo Rights/Permissions Editor
Heidi Giovine: Administrative Manager

Rosen Publishing
Megan Kellerman: Managing Editor
Xina M. Uhl: Editor
Greg Tucker: Creative Director
Brian Garvey: Art Director

Cataloging-in-Publication Data
Names: New York Times Company.
Title: Religious freedom / edited by the New York Times editorial staff.
Description: New York : New York Times Educational Publishing,
2020. | Series: Changing perspectives | Includes glossary and index.
Identifiers: ISBN 9781642822366 (library bound) | ISBN
9781642822359 (pbk.) | ISBN 9781642822373 (ebook)
Subjects: LCSH: Freedom of religion—United States—Juvenile
literature. | Religion and state—United States—Juvenile literature.
Classification: LCC BR516.R455 2019 | DDC 323.44'20973—dc23

Manufactured in the United States of America

On the cover: Although religious freedom was a founding
principle of the United States, it is a multifaceted issue that
remains relevant and widely debated today; Indranil Mukherjee/
AFP/Getty Images.

Contents

CHAPTER 3

Freedom for Different Groups and Sects

CHAPTER 5

Twenty-First Century Issues

Introduction

THE FREEDOM TO LIVE and worship as one pleases is a concept that has come about only after centuries of struggle and strife. The landing of the Pilgrims and the Puritans on American shores, in 1620 and 1630, respectively, established religion and freedom at the heart of the country's European colonization. In 1786, one of the United States' founders, Thomas Jefferson, composed the Virginia Statute for Religious Freedom. It was then passed by the Virginia General Assembly. This statement is considered the precursor of the Constitution's First Amendment protections for religious liberty. It reads in part:

> Be it enacted by the General Assembly, that no man shall be compelled to frequent or support any religious worship, place, or ministry whatsoever, nor shall be enforced, restrained, molested, or burthened [burdened] in his body or goods, nor shall otherwise suffer on account of his religious opinions or belief; but that all men shall be free to profess, and by argument to maintain, their opinion in matters of religion, and that the same shall in no wise diminish, enlarge, or affect their civil capacities.

This philosophy, that all people need not fear religious persecution, remains a founding principle of the United States, one which did not evolve in isolation. Neither was it always strictly adhered to. Religious issues were not the same as those today. Local and state laws regarding the observance of Sunday as a holiday restricted the activities and consumption of citizens, particularly in regards to alcohol. These blue laws had a number of opponents, and were a frequent topic of controversy. However, restrictions on alcohol sales still exist in a number of cities today.

America's willingness to accept various religious groups sometimes caused problems with the law. The Mormons' practice of polygamy,

Schenectady, N.Y., 1973: Students hold a 10-minute prayer session at their public high school. The school board gave permission for the meetings even though the 1963 U.S. Supreme Court decision ruled out prayer in public schools.

the marrying of multiple wives to one husband, was one such problem. Although Mormons attempted to continue this practice on the grounds of religious liberty, the Supreme Court ruled it illegal. Jehovah's Witnesses, the Salvation Army, Quakers and Christian Scientists, in addition to others, ran afoul of certain laws. When it came time to go to war, individuals called "conscientious objectors" cited their religious beliefs prohibiting them from participating in violence. Even the practice of saluting the flag was banned by certain sects.

In the twentieth century, issues of religious freedom continued to cause controversies, such as whether prayer was acceptable in public schools, if public funds could be used to bus students to religious schools and even if religious clubs were allowed to meet on school campuses. Governmental displays of a religious nature were challenged. The authority of the Catholic Church suffered due to numerous sex abuse scandals. Christianity's condemnation of gays and lesbians may even have contributed to the government's slow response to the AIDS epidemic, which at first was seen as a "gay problem."

The modern news also frequently tackles issues of religious liberty. Debate was sparked by the presence of a Ten Commandments monument placed at the Alabama Supreme Court. The Trump administration demonstrated its suspicion against Muslim immigrants with its travel ban. The refusal of a Colorado baker to make a wedding cake for a gay couple even made its way up to the highest court of the land based on arguments involving the freedom of religion. These are only some of the issues that will continue to be explored in the twenty-first century.

CHAPTER 1

The History of Religious Liberty in the United States and Abroad

The history of religious freedom in Europe evolved only after many centuries of power struggles between government and the church. The Reformation that began in 1517 split the Roman Catholic Church. Christianity in Europe now existed in two forms: Catholic and Protestant. This split resulted in violence and intolerance, and it also preceded the development of many Protestant sects. The Puritans were one such sect, and they made a lasting impression on the early American colonies.

Religious Toleration in Mexico — The Progress Made Under Maximilian.

BY THE NEW YORK TIMES | NOV. 21, 1866

FROM SO PRIEST-RIDDEN a country as Mexico, from so devout a religionist as its luckless "Emperor," little was ever hoped in the way of ecclesiastical toleration.

It happens, therefore, that few of our people have taken pains to note how great a change in favor of religious liberty was effected under the auspices of the Prince who is now leaving the scene of his brief adventure. Our own military occupation of Mexico, twenty years ago, left hardly a trace of itself, in any overthrowing of monkish superstition, and none whatever in creating popular respect for the religious beliefs of foreign residents. It was reserved for an army of Frenchmen and Austrians, with all their own prejudices running in an opposite current, to work out this mark of progress in civilization.

On the 10th of June, 1863, the French expeditionary troops, under Marshal Forey, made this triumphal entry into the City of Mexico. Three days previous, Gen. Bazaixe's division, in advance, had entered and taken possession. A very short time thereafter a French army chaplain made application to the military authorities for the assignment of a place in which to hold Protestant worship. The priests, getting wind of his purpose, opposed him in every way; but, in fine, the French commander decided to give him the hall of the College San Ildefonsa.

So far, all was well. But a now difficulty arose — the priests refused to give up the keys. Accordingly, a squad of French Zouaves was sent down, under the command of a nephew of Marshal (then General) Bazaine, with instructions to coerce the priest into obedience. The latter, alarmed at the apparition of bayonets, shifted their tactics, and told Capt. Bazaine they "had lost the keys." The young French officer, in reply, gave three minutes in which to find the keys, promising that at the end of this time, by the watch, if they continued lost, he would break down the doors. The keys were instantly forthcoming.

Thus, literally at the point of the bayonet, religious toleration was secured in the City of Mexico, and possibly some of the same red-legged troops who had lately guarded the honors and privileges of the Sovereign of Borne, may have been among those who forced their way into the College of San Ildefonsa, three thousand miles away. At all events, it was by the order of a French officer servicing that the deed was accomplished. There were outcries of "sacrilege" and "desecration" but soldiers obey orders, and when once the enterprising chaplain had got permission for his services, he got also the French army to back him.

The room thus "confiscated" was full of rubbish of one and another sort, and, it being already Friday, could not be cleaned in season for service on the next Sunday. But for the Sunday after, services were announced. The few Protestants in the city heard the news with strange emotion. Nearly twenty years had gone by since such religious worship had been held in the city; and that which was permitted during the occupation by the American army, was of so brief duration as to seem hardly a break in the long centuries of the dominion of priestcraft there. This was the first attempt to establish permanently a Protestant Church in the heart of the country, and the attempt was successful.

At the first service about twenty persons were present, a good share of whom were connected with the American and English legations. Since that time the same active chaplain has held services regularly every Sunday, and his audience has increased to about one hundred, exclusive of the French troops. Indeed, the congregation grew until it became necessary to remove to a larger hall. A church was established, Lutheran in creed and form of worship, and to it several Mexicans were admitted. The service, of course, is entirely in French; yet most of the audience, outside of the army, are English and Americans, some of whom do not understand the language, but make it a point of duty to lend the religious association the support of their presence.

Among these, Mr. Corwin, the predecessor of Mr. Campbell as our Minister to Mexico, was noted for his regularity of attendance.

Such is the way in which freedom of worship was introduced into the City of Mexico. It is to the credit of the retiring Prince, that, in religion as in some other matters, he showed himself the friend and advocate of toleration. Overtures to Marshal Bazaine to recall the military permission for holding Lutheran services met a prompt and decisive rebuff; recourse to Maximilian was not more successful. This gain to the cause of freedom is the more praiseworthy, because it was given by a Prince whose own convictions were so strongly conservative. Above all, it was given in a country where it seriously risked popularity by offending religious prejudices; and popularity was of all things the one would-be Emperor could not afford to lose.

Some time ago, certain agents of the American Bible Society were seized and their books burned, in several Mexican cities, under an old law preventing the circulation of the common editions of the Scriptures. But Maximilian, on being appealed to, released the agents; and in the capital no such outrage was attempted.

One of the first points to be arranged for by our agents in dealing with Juarez, or any one else representing the Mexican Government, is that we shall have no more nonsense about this matter of the freedom of public worship. We allow every sort of religionist to worship here as he may think fit. There will have to be a reciprocity in this business. The world is getting tired of the other style. Our Government, acting as it probably will do, in concert with that of France, will certainly see that the old system of intolerance comes to a speedy end in the community where we are compelled peaceably to intervene.

Austrian Progress — Religions Liberty — The Press Law in Hungary.

BY THE NEW YORK TIMES | MARCH 26, 1868

THERE HAS ALWAYS BEEN something remarkable in the vitality which has enabled Austria to survive the calamities that have over and over again threatened her with utter ruin and dismemberment. No loss of territory, no financial distress, has ever prevented her from again taking the field as a great Power, when called upon, and no loss of prestige, however unbroken the series of reverses, has ever caused her soldiers to fight with less gallantry. But this power of stolid resistance to external shocks was manifestly not fated to last forever. It was based simply on military force wielded by an absolute power, the identity of which with all that was intolerant in religion and anti-popular in policy was proverbial. The organization of the Austrian Empire had long survived disastrous campaigns and resisted revolution with success; but that it could hold together long in defiance of the all-pervading liberal tendencies of the age, seemed at one time little short of impossible. The idea that Austria could read the signs of the times, and voluntarily set her house in order, was apparently not to be entertained.

But even Hapsburgs learn, and with the loss of her last wrongfully-held possessions in Italy, Austria gained the knowledge that her only hope laid in a contented people and the development of her vast resources. Constitutional reforms have been effected of late with a quietness that is apt to mislead the observer as to their real importance. It is not many years ago since Austria was delivered into the power of the Papacy, bound hand and foot by the terms of an agreement dictated in the very haughtiest spirit of priestly arrogance and bigotry. But now the Concordat stands in the way of popular demands, and we learn by telegraph that in spite of the most determined opposition on the part of the clerical party, the Civil Marriage bill has passed both Houses of the Reichsrath. One of the most vital provisions of the Concordat is thus annulled, and the popular rejoicings of which we hear show how the triumph over the enemies of religious liberty is appreciated. If the whole power of the Papal hierarchy cannot avail to maintain one of the most cherished instruments of ecclesiastical domination — the exclusive control of the marriage contract — there are new and better times coming for the freedom and happiness of the Austrian people.

Another favorable sign for Austria is the apparent solidity of the basis upon which the conciliation of Hungary has been effected, and an event has recently taken place which shows very forcibly the altered state of things. It will be recollected that some months ago Kossuth addressed a letter to a Hungarian paper in which he violently denounced the acceptance by Hungary of the Austrian concessions, and protested against the continuance of any connection whatever with the House of Hapsburg. The editor, a member of the Hungarian Diet, had many thousand free copies circulated. The thing assumed the proportions of an agitation against a regime formally accepted by Hungary, and it was determined to put in force for the first time the Press law granted in Hungary in 1818. Proceedings were taken against the editor, every advantage was given to the accused, and the trial was conducted in accordance with both the spirit and the minutest details of Hungarian law. Finally, a Hungarian jury found a verdict of guilty of an offence against the "King of Hungary," and of agitation against the connexion of the Kingdom and the Austrian Empire, and a severe sentence, though considerably less than the full penalty, was inflicted.

It is certainly a sign of the altered temper of the times when an affair like this, that would lately have called forth some despotic and barbarous mode of repression, and set all Hungary in a blaze, can be settled quietly by constitutional proceedings and the decision of a jury, even when so deadly an enemy of the powers that be as Kossuth is implicated. The situation was a very delicate one. The Hungarian people do not wish to be plunged into further war, and yet the name of Kossuth was surrounded by too many associations for his letter to be passed over in silence. Arbitrary repression would have infallibly resulted in troubles more or less severe; adherence to constitutional forms rendered the whole affair harmless. Napoleon himself, when "crowning the edifice," might have learned a good deal even from Austria.

Religious Liberty in the United States.

BY THE NEW YORK TIMES | APRIL 23, 1876

REV. DR. H. M. DEXTER, of the *Congregationalist,* and, according to the Springfield *Republican,* "one of our best historical experts, especially in New-England matters," has published what the same authority styles "a monograph, at once exhaustive and brilliant," in defense of the scandalous treatment meted out by the Massachusetts colony to Roger Williams. Dr. Dexter was moved by a petition addressed to the Massachusetts Legislature praying for the revocation of the order of banishment passed some 240 years ago, "to deprive the name of Roger Williams of its potency as a controversial red rag and sectarian war cry." The monographist is credited with being "quite thankful to the few excellent — if not erudite" — signers of this curious petition for giving him an opportunity of showing how competent he is to wield the historical whitewash brush. He throws down the gauntlet before the Baptists and the rest of the world, challenging proof that, under all the circumstances, the treatment which Roger Williams received from the General Court of the Massachusetts Bay Colony was not about right. After what we should judge from the Springfield *Republican*'s account to be an extremely one-sided statement of the views which the founder of Rhode Island defended so resolutely, Dr. Dexter closes his indictment with this remarkable statement: "Mr. Williams lived and died in humiliating ignorance of the fact which his biographers and eulogists have since discovered, that 'the head and front of his offending' consisted in his 'maintaining the great doctrine which has immortalized his name: that the civil power has no jurisdiction over the conscience.' "

We imagine that the American Baptist denomination — with whose early history Roger Williams was for a short time identified — contains enough men of real erudition to make very short work of statements which are either the product of sham erudition or gross and invincible prejudice. We propose to attempt less a vindication of the fame and character of the father of religious liberty on this continent than to elucidate some facts connected with the earliest struggle for soul-freedom in the American colonies, which may be found both seasonable and instructive in this Centennial year of American Independence. If these facts can be so grossly misrepresented by a reverent doctor and a "historical expert," what must be the state of mind of the lay and unlearned reader in regard to them?

The "religious freedom for which our fathers fought" has become a stock phrase with patriotic speakers and writers, and people have got into a loose habit of assuming that the struggle for political self-government on this continent was, throughout all its phases, a struggle for the rights of conscience also. This is true to the extent that perfect civil liberty can never be compatible with constraint on account of religious opinion, and that every advance made toward the one makes it less possible to enforce the other. But in the history of the American colonies, as in the history of the mother country, the development of the principles of religious liberty lagged very far behind the growth of clear ideas about civil freedom. The declaration signed in the cabin of the Mayflower contained the germ of American Democracy, but it also took for granted a uniformity of religious opinion in presence of which impartial toleration was impossible. Edward Winslow and his fellow-pilgrims in 1620 were as clearly committed as were John Endicott and his Puritan colonists of 1629 to the enforced maintenance of certain sharply defined forms of church government as a necessary portion of the Constitution of the State. The non-conformists of New-England were as little disposed as the conformists of Virginia to waive their right to exclude from the protection of their charters all who refused to give an unqualified adhesion to the religious system which they had established.

The vast majority of "our fathers," therefore, held opinions directly opposed to the modern American ideal of religious freedom, and the long struggle of a resolute minority against the Old World prepossessions on this subject, from which neither Puritan nor cavalier colonists had emancipated themselves, is one of the most remarkable passages in our history. The heroes of that struggle have certainly failed to receive the full meed of honor due to their courage, their foresight, and their self-denial. How much it needed of all three to sustain the defenders of religious toleration 240 years ago, can only be appreciated by those who have studied the bitterness of controversy, the rigor of legislative enactment, and the hard, unbending social temper which characterized that age. And, further back than these, there must be taken into account the accumulated momentum of a "stream of tendency" which, for ages, had set in favor of the right of the State to enforce religious uniformity. The necessity and defensibility of persecution as a corrective of religious schism had been the unbroken tradition of the Church for nearly twelve centuries. When Constantine placed Christianity under the protection of the State, the means were provided for repressing differences of opinion within the Church by the arm of the flesh, as well as for compelling the submission of obstinate disbelievers or heretics outside of its pale. Two generations after the Church had ceased to furnish martyrs, it began to stamp out heresy by the aid of the public executioner. When the old imperial City of Trier witnessed, in the beheading of Priscillian and his adherents, the first blood shed at the demand of Christian bishops, there were not wanting Christian teachers able to discern the gross inconsistency of the act with the spirit of the teacher of Galilee. Two of the fathers of the fourth century — Martin of Tours and Ambrose of Milan — certainly did protest vehemently against it. But the spirit of intolerance grew so fast that it carried with it, a few years later, even the great and liberal-minded Augustine. This sentence, for example, about the Donatists carries with it the very essence of mediaeval persecution: "They murder souls, and themselves are afflicted in body; they put men to everlasting death, and yet they complain when themselves are put to suffer temporal death."

It is true that the Church, even in the most cruel times, ostentatiously disclaimed all sympathy with the shedding of blood for cause of conscience. *Ecclesia abhorret a sanguine* is a maxim of the canon law, and from the days of the Albigenses to the time of Alva, the ecclesiastic who had judged and condemned an obstinate heretic never forgot, in handing over his victim to the torture or the stake, to give him the benefit of the hypocritical formula by which the Church prayed that he might be spared from all danger of death or mutilation.

The theory was — as Boniface VIII. put it in his famous bull, *Unam Sanctam* — the Church can only wield the sword of the spirit, but then kings and rulers who wield the sword of the flesh are subject to her. The Church does not persecute, she simply exhausts all her powers of remonstrance with obstinate heretics, and, finding them unconvinced, hands them over for punishment to the secular powers. The ecclesiastical authorities held themselves to be as clearly bound to repress false doctrine by the aid of civil penalties as to check, by similar means, the practice of vice and immorality. In fact, the stamping out of heresy was regarded as a much more imperative duty than the preservation of good morals. The soul that believed not, in the orthodox sense of the term, was sure of eternal perdition, whereas there were sundry ecclesiastical remedies provided for purging the immortal part which had been merely defied by immorality or crime.

However earnestly the founders of the Reformed Churches contended for the principle of liberty of conscience, they were as little tolerant as any Romish theologian of what they regarded as pernicious errors. Even the gentle Beza wrote in favor of enforced conformity in doctrinal opinion, and Calvin's ideal of a theocratic state had its logical outcome in the burning of Servetus. But few of those who carried forward the work of Luther paid much heed to his great dictum that "the laws of the civil magistrate's government extend no further than over the body and goods and to that which is external, for over the soul God will not suffer any man to rule." It is not very many years ago since the law was repealed in England which made ecclesiastical excommunication involve the deprivation of civil rights, and as Fitz James Stephen has recently shown, the Ecclesiastical Courts of that country retain to this day, under an unrepealed statute of Charles II., the power to inflict sentences of fine or imprisonment, or both, "for atheism, blasphemy, heresy, or schism, and other damnable doctrines and opinions." But this statute, which has so long survived the state of public opinion to which it owed its birth, was a great advance over preceding legislation on the same subject.

It finally abolished the penalty of capital punishment for heresy which had been inflicted during the reigns of their most Christian and Protestant Majesties, Edward VI., Elizabeth, and James I. These executions had not even the defense of being in conformity with the law of the land. The statute *de heretico comburendo*, passed in the reign of Henry IV. to meet the case of the Lollards, had been repealed under Edward VI., was revived again under Mary, and was finally repealed in the reign of Elizabeth. The executions for heresy sanctioned by the "Bloody Mary" had, therefore, a quality of legality which was wanting in those sanctioned by her Protestant predecessor and successor. James I. was advised by his Judges, Lord Coke dissenting, that the writ *de heretico comburendo* could issue at common law, independently of the repealed statute, very much, to borrow Mr. Froude's illustration, as if a common law writ could enable the Crown to order a man to be executed for sheep-stealing in spite of the long exclusion of that crime from the list of capital offenses. But the truth is, public sentiment in these days was as prone as it had been 200 years before to regard as a crime against society any denial of the fundamental principles of the generally accepted faith. The grounds of religious division had greatly multiplied, but that did not necessarily make men more tolerant. At least it did not prevent them from viewing as a perfectly justifiable exercise of royal authority the putting to death of men who openly repudiated the first principles of Christianity. The Puritans, on whom the hand of unfriendly prelates certainly pressed heavily enough during the reign of the British Solomon, would have indignantly repudiated any connection between the principles for which they contended, and those which were outraged in the burning of Legatt and Wightman for denying the divinity of Christ.

A generation later, the prevailing sentiment in regard to the limits of religious freedom had undergone but little change. The Presbyterians, who mainly composed the Westminster Assembly, were much of the same mind as their Scottish brother, Robert Baylie, who declared "Liberty of conscience and toleration of all or any religion is so prodigious an impiety that this religious parliament cannot but abhor the very meaning of it." The "five dissenting brethren" who represented the Independents at the General Assembly of Divines, and were jealously watching to see whether Presbytery was to be set up *jure divino*, were at least sound, according to the Baylie standard, on the question of religious toleration. Little as he liked these opponents of Presbyterianism, Baylie could not but admit that, "Whatever may be the opinions of John Goodwin, Mr. Williams, and some of that stamp, yet Mr. Burroughs (one of the five Independents) in his late *Irenicum*, upon very unanswerable arguments, explodes that abomination." Robinson, of Leyden, the spiritual father of the Plymouth Colony, wrote against toleration, and among the Puritan colonists of the Bay it was regarded as one of the most pernicious doctrines which had ever been evolved by the perversity of human speculation. After the death of old Gov. Dudley these doggerel lines were found in his pocket, preserved apparently as a kind of amulet against the most dangerous distemper of the age:

> *Let men of God in courts and churches watch,*
> *O'er such as do a toleration hatch;*
> *Lest that ill egg bring forth a cockatrice,*
> *To poison all with heresies and vice.*

Even the clear and well-poised intellect of the elder Winthrop failed to admit the compatibility of religious liberty with the preservation of civil order. Dr. John Cotton, "the patriarch of New-England," exhausted all the resources of a very able and thoroughly trained mind in the effort to reconcile freedom of conscience with the assumed necessity for persecuting men who persisted in error after the Church had reasoned with and warned them. Impetuous spirits like John Endicott — whose seal was a death's-head and cross-bones, with the name of "John Garvad" in a circle around it — did not stop to argue about the matter, but consistently acted on the maxim that the toleration of vice and immorality was a far less dangerous experiment for society than the toleration of religious opinions fundamentally at variance with those which the majority called orthodox.

Civil and Religious Liberty.

BY THE NEW YORK TIMES | FEB. 1, 1874

THE MEETING HELD recently in London to express sympathy with the German Government in its action against the Roman Catholic Church, presented some peculiar anomalies, and in this respect was quite in accord with the aspect of religious questions throughout Europe and America, for there are many curious points in dispute which, from different aspects, seem to be quite irreconcilable. Here the majority of the people demand that the Bible shall not be excluded from the public schools. In England, a huge section of the dissenters insist that the Bible is not necessary in the public schools. The American theory stands essentially upon the basis of religion and morality. The nonconformists of England base their demands on a spirit of resistance to the Anglican Church, which, under a system of denominational teaching, can always exercise a dominant power. On the principle of absolute religious liberty, we in America leave the churches free to govern their own affairs. Professing the same principle the despotism of Prussia and the Republic of Switzerland have developed a spirit of intolerance to the Roman Catholics which seems to go far beyond the political character of their Church, and rather aims to regulate internal government. And now Lord Russell, with Mr. Newdegate and a few other Parliamentary notabilities, give moral support to that policy, also in the name of civil and religious liberty.

From this aspect the subject is full of interest, and far exceeds in extent the limitation of any simple controversy between Romanism and Protestantism. To make liberty the plea for oppression is at first sight a very peculiar idea, quite at variance with ordinary notions. But is there any oppression in this instance and if so, is it justified? With whatever term we may choose to describe the action of the Swiss and German Governments, both of them offer as a justification the political influence of the Roman Church. They war not against Romanism as a religious belief, but against Romanism as a political power. But Germany once very solemnly declared that she fought not against France, but against Napoleon III. And yet we did not see that the strife was at an end when Napoleon fell. It is possibly in the same way that Prussia and Switzerland have carried the contest, beyond the political limits of the Church, and if so we do not understand how their policy can be defended on the score of religious belief. Very much, therefore, turns upon the nature of Governmental action in the two instances. As the policy of Bismarck has admittedly been more severe than that, adopted by Switzerland, we will look to the latter for some illustrations. It will be conceded that a church has a right to elect its own ministers. No congregation would be satisfied to have the National Government appointing a minister to their church, and that minister a member of some other religious denomination. But this is what the Swiss authorities are doing with the Roman Catholics. In the Bernese Jura and in the canton of Geneva the parish priests have, one and all, been removed from their chapels, and their pulpits have been filled by the appointees of the civil power. Those priests are now in a state of destitution, and their congregations are largely forced to attend the ministration of men whose faith they do not hold.

The change is made in direct violation of the wishes of the people, and is being sustained by the bayonet in the hands of the civil authorities; while the only persons who can be found to fill the vacant places are men who have been expelled from their former benefices for bad conduct. The persecution does not end here. Ostensibly the parish priests are permitted to gather their flocks into barns, or under any shelter they can find, and there to exercise their ministerial functions — a permission which, if the whole policy rest upon political considerations, must surely be as dangerous as the former custom of letting them meet in their respective churches. But the alleged liberty is, in truth, no liberty at all. For priests are arrested and imprisoned on the most trivial pretenses. In one instance the charge was "baptizing an infant in sacerdotal habits," and a fine and imprisonment were inflicted. In another case an entire section of the congregation were seized on a charge of robbery, and after three weeks' imprisonment they were released without any trial or explanation. Many persons have been fined and imprisoned, for not having saluted the newly-appointed ministers in the public streets. In another instance, a couple who had been married by their parish priest were arrested and imprisoned for living in a state of concubinage.

All this is going on under the rule of the Swiss Republic. We are assured that matters are much worse under the iron hand of the German despotism. Nor is religious liberty the only plea put forward in extenuation of this policy. The interests of Protestantism are also alleged but the futility of legislative resistance to religious belief has been brought home to no modern statesman more closely than to Lord Russell. His own efforts to check the influence of the Roman Church in England were utterly ridiculous as well as useless, while they did operate to bring some odium upon the Protestant section of the people. And so it always has been and will be. No church can be wiped out of existence by oppression. The congregations who are now driven out of their chapels in Germany and Switzerland have not changed their convictions nor their ecclesiastical allegiance. It is much more probable that the majority of them are strengthened in both, and thus the cause of Protestantism, as well as that of religious liberty, suffers from the misdirected zeal of their advocates. Lord Russell and his friends would have been more wise if they had abstained from meddling with German home policy, instead of identifying themselves with a movement which is made under false pretenses, and is contrary to the tolerant spirit of the age.

Church and State in Europe.

BY THE NEW YORK TIMES | DEC. 14, 1874

EUROPE DOES NOT PRESENT a picture of the happy family. There is much jarring and bickering and wrangling about many questions on which vital interests are staked. Everywhere may be noticed a more or less unsettled state of affairs, a lowering of the moral standard, a confusion of ideas and principles. This confusion is nowhere more at variance with the supposed enlightenment of the age, than in regard to questions connected with religious freedom, and bearing on the relations of Church and State. There is now scarcely a single country in Europe, in which the evil is not breaking out in one form or another. Italy has, for centuries, been like a body whose soul was the Church. The great political changes which took place there within the present generation have naturally caused a sudden displacement and disruption of interests. The spirit of harmony and peace could not soon be expected to adjust the many claims which were urged in contradiction of one another. The Church was accustomed to rule, spiritually and temporally; she has not yet thought fit to acknowledge any other supremacy. Defiant she stands, and it would be difficult to say how or when she will be brought to terms, or propose any that may be acceptable to the civil Government. In France, the principle of religious liberty has long ago been proclaimed but the tradition of governmental interference and meddlesomeness has outlived the tyranny of State religion. The State has still an influence over the Church, and the Church has a power in State affairs which continually opens a way for all sorts of abuse and mischief. Religious liberty and political freedom are equally at peril through the encroachment of civil or ecclesiastical authority. The latter exerts an undue action on French politics, and the so-called Ultramontane Party has played, and may yet play, an important and not altogether desirable part in the destinies of the country.

Prince Bismarck, also known as Otto von Bismarck, Chancellor of the German Empire, in the Reichstag with his deputies in 1871. On his left is Count Lerchenfeld and on his right, Freiherr von Stengel.

The attitude of the German Government on the question of Church and State is still more perplexing. Germany actually fights over again the battles of the Reformation, but in the wrong direction. Prince Bismarck clutches the power which was wrested from Rome, his State inquisition does not proceed quite so unceremoniously and cruelly as the theocratic inquisition of the Middle Ages, but it is still an inquisition and abuse of power. When his hired evangelical professors try to demonstrate that the state wields the sword of right, and can legally shape ecclesiastical hierarchy and authority according to its caprice and interest. They simply deny the principle of free thought, and, it may be assumed, in contradiction to the great reformers of old. When these champions of religion fought against Papal supremacy, they did not intend to do so for the sake of the divine right of royalty. It is a question whether the Vaterland would be a gainer by accepting the infallibility of Prince Bismarck in place of the dogma proclaimed four years ago by the Vatican Council. That, in the political evolution of the age, nations should sometimes be at a loss in handling newly-acquired instruments of action and progress, that they should often prove to be inexperienced, awkward, and inadequate in the discharge of new duties and the exercise of new rights, that the field of politics should be a field of battle where a thousand hostile opinions and interests meet and clash — all this is quite natural. The political world is full of accidents and surprises. The problems to be solved there admit of various constructions, and the cases at issue, such as a form of government or a course of policy, are liable to be determined by a variety of circumstances. It is not astonishing that men should differ in the view they take in regard to them. But it is astonishing that they should misapprehend or forget what it is to practice religious liberty, and what these words imply, particularly in regard to others.

What we behold in Germany, in Italy, even in free Switzerland, where civil authority has assumed the power of deposing and expelling Ultramontane priests, is not calculated to reflect much credit on their leading men. If they are the true representatives of their age, if their standard of justice is not below that of which we measure the actions of other men and our own, we need not feel very proud of modern progress and civilization. Marvelous and vast as it appears to be, there is yet little security in it for genuine tolerance and freedom. There are still in its wake many relics of barbarity. One of the worst is religious intolerance, religious persecution. It is equally odious, whatever be its origin and whatever its pretext.

Lord Russell and Religious Liberty.

BY THE NEW YORK TIMES | MAY 29, 1878

THE LONDON SATURDAY REVIEW of May 11 said: "At the age of 86 Lord Russell can look back to the day when, 50 years ago, he had the glory of carrying the repeal of the Test and Corporation acts; and a deputation of those who, or whose fathers, have most benefited by his exertions have waited on him to profess the gratitude and respect which this remote passage in his history awakes in their minds. Unfortunately, Lord Russell's health did not permit him to go through the fatigue of receiving personally those who came to do him honor, but Lady Russell answered for him so well that the deputation had every reason to be satisfied. The bulk of the English public would also be quite ready to testify its feelings in favor of Lord Russell as the apostle of religious liberty, were it not that religious liberty has become so familiar to all Englishmen that it is hard to realize a state of things when it did not exist. That the Church can thrive and thrive much better, without excluding members of other communions from their fair share in political and municipal life, has sunk from a discovery into a truism.

Like many things, however, which now seem as if their contraries were impossible, the reign of religious liberty took some trouble to establish. Fortunately for his fame, Lord Russell associated himself more conspicuously and more successfully than anyone else with its establishment. Few would pronounce Lord Russell a great statesman, and fewer still would defend his treatment of his colleagues; but Lord Russell has associated his name with the passing of great measures, and, therefore, even 50 years after the time of his first triumph, the memory of his services is still green. In the conduct and passing of these measures he displayed many high qualities — courage, tenacity, and a hearty genuineness of conviction. He believed, with an almost Mohammedan fervor, in himself and his cause and his high social position, his power in debate and his command over his followers, gave him a force which prevented any cause he espoused from being lightly treated. Had he never lived, it is inconceivable that we should still be degrading the Sacrament into a barrier against Dissenters acting as Mayors. But some one must have arisen to embody and direct an inevitable movement; and few English politicians can be named who were calculated to do his own peculiar work so well as Lord Russell. For, among his other gifts, he had a conspicuous power of forcing the hands of his adversaries. He made them attend to him. He conquered laziness and apathy, and would never allow that his measures could be postponed.

It was Lord Russell's merit that, by erecting civil and religious liberty into a principle which could be felt if it could not be defined, he made small things seem great, and obliged the indifferent and apathetic to face in each case the question why his principle should not prevail. The history of the Test and Corporation acts is one of the most curious parts of the general history of England. That they should have been passed is not so very singular. They were considered, and perhaps rightly considered, as a valuable instrument for the establishment of the Church of England as a political body, and were in keeping with all of the time.

Lord Russell contributed more than any one else to the repeal of those acts, and he continued for years in different shapes the work then begun. But it was his good luck to have to deal with religious liberty in its simplest form. So long religious liberty means the removal of oppression it is plain sailing. But when oppression has been removed, the very difficult question arises, what is meant by the liberty that ought to be accorded to religion if in some ways there is more religious liberty in France than in England. The State pays ministers of different religions; and it is quite a tenable proposition that one of the most valued liberties of the ministers of religion is the liberty of existing. Some of the most conspicuous members of the present French Ministry are Protestants; while it is almost hopeless for a Roman Catholic to present himself to an English or a Scotch constituency. On the other hand, there is much greater liberty of religious discussion

A portrait of Lord Russell.

in England. It is conceivable that a prophet should arise here, but he would be oppressed at once as a nuisance by the French Police. The Liberation Society, again, protests that the very existence of an Established Church is an offense against religious liberty. Why, it may be replied, should not the nation have that amount of liberty in religion which will enable it to have an Established Church if it likes to have one? In point of fact, almost every old country does wish to have an Established Church, if it can only get one without the ministers of the church interfering too much in politics. To force an Established Church on an unwilling population, as the Stuarts forced the Episcopal Church on Scotland, or as Russia forces its peculiar type of the Greek Church on schismatics, is, no doubt, a grave offense against religious liberty. But that a population which wishes for an Established Church should have it, provided the Established Church does not subject those who dissent from it to any civil pains or disabilities, is only to accord to this population the form of religious liberty it desires. The establishment of such a Church is not an offense against religious liberty, but against religious equality, which is quite a different thing. Whether absolute religious equality is desirable is open to fair questioning, like every part of the actual constitution of society; but at any rate it was not in the cause of religious equality that Lord Russell strove and carried the nation with him. His was the narrow but creditable task of removing gross abuses. It has not been his lot, and it was probably not within the range of his powers, to decide the opinion of his countrymen as to what was to be done when these abuses were removed.

A Fruit of Civilization

BY THE NEW YORK TIMES | NOV. 22, 1894

"RELIGIOUS TOLERATION" WAS the subject of a lecture delivered by George Parsons Lathrop in the Madison Square Concert Hall last night, under the auspices of the Catholic Club.

President Seth Low of Columbia College presided, and among those seated with him on the platform were Chief Justice Joseph Daly of the Court of Common Pleas, who is the President of the club; Archbishop Corrigan, Judge Morgan J. O'Brien, Oscar Straus, Dorman B. Eaton, Edward Lauterbach, Rabbi Gustav Gottheil, Myer Stern, the Rev. James M. King, Dr. Da Costa, the Rev. Henry Newey, Fathers Doyle and O'Keefe of the Paulist Fathers, Fathers Hart, Hughes, and Healy, and C. V. Fornes.

Judge Daly made a brief speech of welcome on behalf of the club, and referred to the presence of Archbishop Corrigan, speaking of him as one who is loved and revered by all, and who enjoys the fullest confidence of the community. It is the fondest wish of the Archbishop, he said, that in peace and concord should flourish, in this city and country.

Judge Daly introduced President Low, who said that as a Protestant he thought it a very high compliment to be called upon to preside at an assemblage of the Catholic Club, and when he received the invitation he looked upon it as a command, as every good citizen should be constrained to do whatever is in his power to foster harmony and concord among the many discordant elements in this country. Every one is entitled to free thought, free speech, and freedom to worship God according to the dictates of his conscience, he said.

The lecturer of the evening was then introduced. He said that President Eliot of Harvard recently declared that toleration in religion was the chief moral cause of permanence in the American Republic. Quoting this, Mr. Lathrop pointed out that widespread secret movements for the proscription of Catholic Americans had just caused the people, for the first time in forty years, to pass through a political campaign filled with acrid discussion concerning the oldest form of Christian faith and the millions of Americans who hold to it.

"If the boast of this secret, masked society is true," Mr. Lathrop said, "that they have a membership of 3,000,000, then, indeed, is one of our vaunted principles, religious toleration, written in water."

Speaking of toleration in this country and Europe, Mr. Lathrop said:

There is a good deal of sham tolerance in this country which is near indifferentism. It may be questioned whether genuine tolerance is as widespread here as in Europe. In the greatest and most advanced countries there neither Protestants nor Catholics think it necessary to sneer at each other on account of their religious beliefs, nor are Catholics looked down upon as inferiors by nature or by faith. The true, independent toleration is practically shown in Ireland, where constituencies wholly Catholics have for fifteen years past overwhelmingly elected Protestants to represent them in Parliament, notwithstanding the wormwood memories of wrongs in the past and the still intolerant hostility of some of their countrymen.

The welfare of the Nation depends on the conscience of our fellow-citizens, as well as on our own. To attempt to coerce the sincere conscience in religion is futile. The Catholic Church strictly forbids that any one be forced to accept the faith, and her doctors have written strongly against using any but peaceful means of overcoming error. The right to apply force even to her recalcitrant children is no part of faith in the Catholic Church.

When religious innovations in the Old World attacked her civil rights, seizing her church edifices and suppressing her worship by violence, she had to call in the help of the secular arm, as any citizens had the right to call upon the law for protection. Her antagonists themselves had removed the conflict from the spiritual to the secular field. If any one of the denominations in this country were to be similarly attacked to-morrow, it would undoubtedly call upon the Government for protection in the same way.

Mr. Lathrop spoke of the political toleration of religion established by law in the United States as almost ideal. "It may be well for those who are trying to impair or destroy the equal rights of fellow-citizens," he said, "to remember that they are thereby aiming an axe at their own." He added:

> Political toleration of religion is a fruit of civilization. To attribute it to the last 400 years is to ignore the history of more than three-quarters of our era. The soil from which civilization sprung was filled with life by the Catholic Church, for there was then no other Christianity. The source and continuing force of all our political or social toleration in religion is the doctrine of universal brotherhood, which was preached and enacted into human institutions by the Catholic Church for 1,500 years before the movement of the sixteenth century. And this is preached and enacted by it now with undiminished fervor. Toleration has come to maturity, not from the inherent tendency of that movement, but along with it.
>
> Where was the first great exhibition of toleration? In France, a Catholic country, so early as the end of the sixteenth century. There, by the Edict of Nantes, complete liberty was accorded to the Huguenots, but it was revoked nearly a hundred years after on the charge that they abused it by burning Catholic villages, destroying churches and convents, murdering women and children, or carrying them off captive. The spiritual heirs of those who forced Louis XIV to it cherish indignation at the revocation, but say little or nothing about these charges. Even earlier than the Edict of Nantes, Maximilian II, a Catholic sovereign, sheltered Protestants in Hungary, Austria, and Bohemia, and Matthias, following him in that empire, granted religious liberty to all sects in 1609, nearly ten years before that terrible war of thirty years, which was to renew religious strife among the peoples. Since the close of that war no persecution of Protestants has taken place. But did persecution of Catholics cease?

Mr. Lathrop referred to recent acts of intolerance against Catholics in some parts of Europe, and said:

> In the annals of recent intolerance, Prussia also comes to the front with the Kultur-kampf, or "battle of civilization," undertaken by Bismarck expressly to deprive the Church of liberty, and unite her to the state as a slave. Thousands were exiled and millions left without spiritual ministration. The German Catholics met the persecution with Parliamentary weapons and constitutional agitation only, but for the first time the Iron Chancellor met his match. They overcame the most absolute statesman and the strongest military power on earth.

An engraved portrait of American poet George Parsons Lathrop.

It had been a "battle of civilization" indeed; but the civilization was on the side or religious tolerance. Bismarck publicly acknowledged his mistake to the Reichstag, confessing, in his own words, that "the Catholic Church is not a foreign institution, but a universal institution; and therefore it is a German institution for German Catholics." This is the most recent great persecution, closing only in 1883.

The United States is the first example of a State founded on religious toleration. But this example is not due to the Puritans, who cruelly persecuted all who differed from them, nor to the Episcopalian settlers of Virginia, who adopted against the Catholics the penal code of old England. Religious liberty and toleration were first set up in this glorious country of ours by Catholics, in the Catholic colony of Maryland, as the very basis of the State, by Lord Baltimore. In a short time the Puritans, who had been welcomed there, got the upper hand and passed stringent laws against their Catholic hosts. Then the Anglicans came in, and imposed the cruel British penal code of disfranchisement and oppression on those Maryland Catholics who were the founders of religious liberty in this country. Then, with the struggle against Great Britain, came the act of emancipation for Catholics in 1774, and the principle thus recognized was afterward made firm in our National Constitution.

Yet there have since been several attempts to strip Catholics of their liberties again. In the "thirties" and the "forties" preposterously named "American" parties were formed, that pillaged Catholic settlements, burned churches and convents according to the fine old foreign custom, and committed many murders. Then, in 1853, came the Know-Nothing Party, which left a trail of proscription, mobs, murders, and destruction. And now we have the A. P. A., the Bashi Bazouks of a new anti-Catholic raid.

The Catholic doctrine of government has always been that all power is from God, and the power of self-government in man is by divine right.

The lecturer pointed out at some length that the only real unions of Church with State had been effected by Protestants, who joined the spiritual hardship with the temporal, in the one person of the secular sovereign, as in Sweden, Norway, Denmark, Prussia, and England; or vested the two faculties of secular and spiritual rule in the members and ministers of the Church, that thus became the State as in the Massachusetts colony. That model has been discarded by the Republic. Leo XIII., in the encyclical on the Christian state, he said, expounded the innate difference and separate functions of the State and the Church. Catholics have not sought a union of Church and State; they do not now, and they never will.

The closing part of the lecture was devoted to showing how the Catholic Church has been and is the fostering friend of education. Finally Mr. Lathrop urged that true and practical toleration should be taught by every Church as a matter of good citizenship, the first duty of every citizen, and the first principle of the written Constitution guaranteeing religious liberty to all men. He asked that all honest members of society should work toward this end, in the name of the Republic, "that these United States may not bring a blot upon the splendor of modern civilization."

CHAPTER 2

The Effect of Religion on Laws

Local and state laws often required that Sunday be observed as a religious holiday. The sale of liquor and tobacco products was often prohibited. Various businesses like restaurants, barber shops, entertainment venues and others were often mandated to be closed. Supporters of such Sunday laws, also called blue laws, argued that observance of religious holidays made for better public morals. Supporters also argued that working people should have a day off. Jews objected to Sunday laws since their time of worship is from Friday evening until Saturday sundown, not on Sunday as it is for Christians. Sunday laws often resulted in both arrests and protests. Blue laws still exist in a number of communities today.

Shall We Have a Sabbath?

BY THE NEW YORK TIMES | OCT. 17, 1867

THE ENFORCEMENT OF the Sunday section of the Metropolitan Excise Law has aroused a most persistent opposition on the part of those who have felt its restraints, and they avow a determination to support no candidate for office who will not pledge himself to use his influence to repeal the clause prohibiting the traffic in liquor on Sunday. The pressure to this end has been so powerful that the recent conduct of political partisans justifies the apprehension that efforts will be made to repeal the law.

The misrepresentations by a part of the public Press, and especially by the German secular papers, in regard to the law and the efforts to enforce it, have been calculated to mislead the public, and create a false impression. The spirit of the anti-Sunday movement, and the tone of the Press which assails the law, are shown by the following extracts, which give a fair view of the character of the opposition.

At a German Anti-Sabbath meeting in Chicago, Aug. 17, 1867, the principal speaker said: "On Sundays we ascend the hills of social pleasures, and drown our troubles in good beer and fiery wine, and forget all the cares of life." Resolutions were adopted at several German Anti-Sabbath and Anti-Temperance meetings last summer, "That they will never vote for any man who is in favor of Sunday and temperance laws."

The New-York *Demokrat*, a German daily paper, winds up a series of recent Anti-Sunday articles with the repeated demand: "Equality of rights for all. No caste of priests! Either abolish the observance of Sunday as a public institution altogether, or close the churches on Sunday." The same paper, Oct. 11, 1867, says: "It is notorious that the Americans are afflicted with the 'English disease,' which is a religious madness composed of pietism, Phariseeism, hypocrisy, Sunday sanctimoniousness and humbug, and supported by downright fanaticism."

A petition was presented June 23, 1867, to the Constitutional Convention of this State, urging that the "reading of the Bible in the public schools be prohibited by the Constitution, and all Sabbath laws be abolished. The German Central Republican Committee of New-York sent a petition to the same Convention to the effect "that Sabbatarian and Temperance legislation be forever banished from the statute book;" and declared "that they will never vote for a revised Constitution which sanctions such laws."

The New-York Sabbath Committee and the friends of the Christian Sabbath have felt a deep interest in the enactment and enforcement of the law which prohibits traffic in liquor on Sunday, and they are so fully satisfied with its beneficent results that the Committee deem it their duty to declare that its repeal would be a public calamity, and they urge the friends of the Sabbath to make efforts to sustain the law.

It is alleged that the law interferes with civil and religious liberty. This charge is utterly groundless. It simply prohibits the public traffic in liquor and beer on Sundays. Beyond this it neither restrains nor interferes with the conduct of any one, provided the people are undisturbed in their enjoyment of a day of quiet rest. Its opponents endeavor to create an impression that the restraints of the law are harsh and rigid beyond precedent. That this charge is entirely false is shown by the following facts:

Sunday traffic in intoxicating drinks has been prohibited by State and municipal laws, which have been enacted from time in time for more than two hundred years. In 1855 the following City ordinance was passed:

If any person in the City of New-York shall sell by retail, or deliver, in pursuance of any such sale, any wine, ale, lager-beer, or other strong or spirituous liquor, or shall consent to allow or permit any wine, ale, lager-beer, or other strong or spirituous liquor by him or her so sold and delivered, to be drank in his or her house, outhouse, garden or other premises whatsoever, without being licensed according in law, or, being so licensed, shall sell or deliver, or consent to allow or permit any wine, ale, lager-beer or other strong or spirituous liquor sold or delivered as aforesaid, to be drank as aforesaid on the first day of the week called Sunday, excepting to boarders and lodgers or actual travelers, within the provisions of the law, he or she shall for every such offence be liable to the pains and penalties hereinafter mentioned.

Approved March 20, 1855, by
> *FERNANDO WOOD, Mayor.*

It should be observed that this ordinance prohibits the sale of wine, ale and lager-beer on Sunday, as well as other strong drinks.

In delivering the opinion of the Supreme Court upon the constitutionality of Sunday laws in 1861, Judge William F. Allen says:

As a civil and political institution, the establishment and regulation of a Sabbath is within the just power of the civil government. Older than our Government the framers of the Constitution did not abolish, alter, or

weaken its sanction, but recognized, as they might otherwise have estab-
lished it. All interests require national uniformity in the day observed,
and that its observance should be so far compulsory as to protect those
who desire and are entitled to the day.

As a civil institution, the sanction of the day is at the option of the
Legislature; but it is fit that the Christian Sabbath should be observed
by a Christian people, and it does not detract from the moral or legal
sanction of a statute that it conforms to the law of God, as recognized by
the great majority of the people. Existing here by common law, all that the
Legislature attempts to do is to regulate its observance. The common law
recognizes the day. Contracts, land redemption, &c., maturing on Sunday,
must be performed on Saturday or Monday. Judicial acts on the Sabbath
are mostly illegal. Work done on Sunday cannot be recovered for, &c.

The Christian Sabbath is, then, one of the civil institutions of the State,
to which the business and duties of life are by the common law made
to conform and adapt themselves. Nor is it a violation of the right of
conscience of any that the Sabbath of the people, immemorially enjoyed,
sanctioned by common law, and recognized in the Constitution, should be
respected and protected by the law-making power.

The existence of the Sabbath as a civil institution being conceded, as
it must be, the right of the Legislature to control and regulate it and its
observance is a necessary sequence. Precedents are found in the statutes
of every government, really or nominally Christian, from the period of
Athelstan to the present day.

It is the right of the citizen to be protected from offences against
decency, and against acts which tend to corrupt the morals and debase
the moral sense of the community. It is the right of the citizen that the
Sabbath as a civil institution, should be kept in a way not inconsistent
with its purpose and the necessity out of which it grew as a day of rest
rather than as a day of riot and disorder, which would be to overthrow it
and render it a curse rather than a blessing.

Judge Wright, in delivering the unanimous opinion of the Court of
Appeals, Dec. 31, 1866, pronounces the present Excise Law "a more
liberal Excise Law than that which it supercedes, or any general law
since the organization of the Government, as a part of its police system, regulating, restraining and prohibiting the traffic in intoxicating
drinks," and adds:

The act assailed is simply regulatory of the retail traffic in intoxicating liquors, and less rigorous as a scheme of regulation than any in force within the limits of the State for more than half a century. The right to legislate on a subject so deeply affecting the public welfare and security has not heretofore been questioned or denied; and it could not well be, for it would have been to deny the power of government inherent in every sovereignty to the extent of its dominions. A State is not sovereign without the power to regulate all its internal commerce as well as police. It is a bold assertion, at this day, that there is any thing in the State or United States Constitutions conflicting with or setting bounds upon the legislative discretion or action, in directing how, when and where a trade shall be conducted in articles intimately connected with the public morals or public safety or public prosperity; or indeed, to prohibit and suppress such traffic altogether, if deemed essential to effect those great ends of good government.

Prior to this Excise Law, there were in the Metropolitan Police District 9,250 liquor shops and beer saloons, of which 8,600 were not licensed. Under this law the grocery stores no longer retail liquor, and it has diminished the number of liquor shops by more than 3,000, and those of the worst class, which were largely supported by Sunday dissipation, and which filled the prisons and poor-houses with victims of intemperance.

The law has diminished the number of arrests on Sundays nearly one-half, and reduced the labors of the Police accordingly. On the fifteen Sundays following the second Sunday in January, 1867, when the law began to be enforced, the number of arrests for intoxication and disorderly conduct were 718 less than on the corresponding Sundays of 1866 under the old system. On the eight Sundays in July and August last, the number of arrests for the same offences amounted to 412 against 831 during the nine Sundays in July and August, 1866.

Formerly there were more cases of drunkenness on Sunday than on any other day of the week. The contrary is the case under the new law, as appears by the following return received at the Metropolitan Police Headquarters. It is shown that for the ten weeks succeeding the 10th of August last the number of arrests for the several days of the week had averaged as follows: Monday, 295; Tuesday, 280; Wednesday, 250; Thursday, 280; Friday, 225; Saturday, 342; while on Sunday the arrests were only 165.

Neither can the citizens of the Metropolitan Police District, burdened with taxes largely increased by pauperism and crime resulting from the traffic in liquor, overlook the financial results of this law, which in two years has contributed nearly $2,600,000 for their relief.

The friends of good order and Christianity may well be aroused when political partisans consent to tamper with laws which protect the rights of the community. If this law, which has been so great a blessing to this City, is destroyed, it is morally certain that other cities and towns throughout the State and nation must look for unrestrained traffic in liquor on Sunday and the deplorable results which will follow.

Let the friends of good order, by their acts and voice, show that the Sabbath shall not be lost without a manly effort to save it.

Our people will not adopt the continental Sunday. We give our immigrant population a cordial welcome to our shores. They have the protection of our laws, but they must not disregard them or offensively violate time-honored and cherished national customs, so intimately connected with our institutions as a Christian people.

Many of the better class of immigrants are in hearty sympathy with our institutions. German mass meetings in favor of our Sunday laws were held in this year in New-York, Williamsburg, Brooklyn, Buffalo, Chicago, Milwaukee and other cities, in which pastors and churches of all denominations took part. At the German meeting in Cooper Institute, the new Excise Law was unanimously sustained by the following resolution:

Resolved, That with the vast majority of our American fellow-citizens, we cordially approve of the new Metropolitan Excise Law as a wholesome and necessary restraint upon the evils of intemperance and Sabbath profanation, and demand for it a fair trial in the full conviction that, according to the experience of the last few Sabbaths, it will, by its fruits fully justify itself to all the friends of order and good morals, even among those who are now opposed or indifferent to it.

In view of these facts, we earnestly urge the friends of good order to stand up for the cause of the Christian Sabbath at this critical period in its history. The eternal principles of morality and religion are of vastly more importance to the country than political party measures which change and pass away with shifting events. Any political party which takes a stand against our Christian institutions can only injure itself, and will be repudiated before long by a Christian people. The high and holy duty of legislators is, by wise laws, to protect the rights, to elevate the character, and to promote the true moral and physical welfare of a people. Hence the best men with the best principles should be chosen for the offices of public trust. Exert your influence as citizens to this end by individual effort, and through the pulpit and the press. If the Christians of this land do their duty as good citizens, they will save the Republic from moral decay, and avert from us so great a calamity as the overthrow of our American Christian Sabbath.

New-York Sabbath Committee;

NORMAN WHITE, *Chairman.*

NATHAN BISHOP,	WM. A. BOOTH,
ROBERT CARTER,	THOMAS C. DOREMUS,
JOHN ELLIOTT,	FRED G. FOSTER,
JOHN C. HAVEMEYER,	DAVID HOADLEY,
JNO. E. PARSONS,	DANIEL L. ROSS,
GUSTAV SCHWAB,	WM. A. SMITH,
JONATHAN STURGES,	OTIS D. SWAN,
WM. WALKER,	F. S. WINSTON,

O. E. WOOD.

JAMES W. BEEKMAN, *Recording Secretary.*

PHILIP SCHAFF, *Corresponding Secretary.*

J. M. MORRISON, *Treasurer.*

Imprisonment of a Young Woman in New-York for Turning Protestant.

BY THE NEW YORK TIMES | JULY 11, 1868

A CASE OF THE deepest interest to Protestants as well as Catholics, and involving principles of religious liberty as well as of parental jurisdiction, was decided by Judge Sutherland, in the Supreme Court of the State, in this City, yesterday. The circumstances will be found reported in detail in our legal columns. A young woman of Catholic paternity and training was converted from the Roman Church to the Protestant faith. She was a person of good character, excellent conduct, intelligence, and strong convictions. Shortly after she had become a member of the Methodist denomination, her father had her arrested for the offence, and incarcerated in a Catholic institution, known as the "House of the Good Shepherd," — an institution which has a department called the Reformatory Department, the inmates of which are forcibly detained and disciplined for the benefit of their souls. A few days ago, some friends of the girl attempted to secure her release on a writ of *habeas corpus*; and she was brought from the institution to the Court. She reiterated her renunciation of Catholicity and her adhesion to Protestantism, and expressed her anxiety to return to the friends who had protected her. Her father, however, declared she was a wayward girl, and that it was to keep her from evil that he had put her under restraint, by confinement in the Catholic institution.

After the hearing of evidence and argument, Judge Sutherland decided that the writ must be dismissed, and the prisoner remanded to the custody of the House of the Good Shepherd. Thereupon she was taken out of Court by her custodians, evidently (according to our reporter) "in a very distressed state of mind."

A Blow at Polygamy.

BY THE NEW YORK TIMES | JAN. 8, 1879

GEORGE REYNOLDS, a member of the Church of the Latter Day Saints, Utah, was indicted in the Third Judicial District Court of that Territory for bigamy. He did not deny that he had more than one wife. But he set up in defense, when brought to trial, that the statute of the United States prohibiting bigamous marriages was unconstitutional and void. He also pleaded that, according to the practice of the Latter Day Saints, polygamous marriages were expressly sanctioned as of divine origin, and that a plurality of wives was divinely ordained. It was alleged that the Constitution of the United States expressly prohibited any interference with polygamy, as a religious rite, in the clause which declares that "Congress shall make no law respecting an establishment of religion, or prohibiting the free exercise thereof." The right to engage in polygamous marriages being embraced in the articles of the Mormon faith, George Reynolds, in his defense, claimed that the United States statute of 1863 was in direct contravention of the above-quoted clause of the Constitution. Nevertheless, the District Court found him guilty of bigamy. He appealed to the Supreme Court of Utah Territory, which tribunal affirmed the judgment of the court below. The case was then taken to the United States Supreme Court on a writ of error, the plaintiff Reynolds pleading, as before, the unconstitutionality of the law of 1862, prohibiting bigamous marriages, the justification of religious belief, and various unimportant legal technicalities. The court decided that the act of Congress prohibiting bigamous marriages was constitutional. Therefore the judgment of the two lower courts was affirmed, and George Reynolds must pay the full penalty of the law.

This is the first decided victory for those who have endeavored to enforce the United States statute leveled against polygamy. By various obvious means, the Mormon residents of Utah were long able to prevent any local court from convicting any person of bigamy. It was not until the machinery of these courts had been changed, and the population of the Territory had become largely anti-Mormon, that a conviction was possible. The statute of 1862 was enacted for the purpose of furnishing a weapon with which to beat down polygamy in Utah. It provided that "every person having a husband or wife living, who marries another, whether married or single, in a Territory, or other place over which the United States have exclusive jurisdiction, is guilty of bigamy, and shall be punished by a fine of not more than $500, and shall be imprisoned for a term of not more than five years." The statute, it will be observed, takes no cognizance of polygamy, or plural marriages. It is confined exclusively to bigamy. The having of two wives is an offense, which, under the law, cannot be aggravated by the having of six or sixteen wives. It is not strictly correct to call bigamy the offense of having a plurality of wives. For, according to the highest authorities, in the canon law bigamy was the marrying of two virgins successively, or one after the death of the other. Nevertheless, in common law, a bigamous person is one who has two or more husbands or wives living, and the name of the offense is not changed when it is proved that the offender has more than two living wives. The statute of 1862, while it was obviously directed at the polygamous practices of the Mormons, merely extended over the Territories the common law in relation to bigamy which exists in every State of the Union.

The Mormons have shown much ingenuity in their management of this peculiar feature of their religious faith and practice. Bigamy, as it is commonly understood among men, they do not hesitate to stigmatize as a crime, if it be practiced by non-Mormons. But when this becomes the act of a person stimulated by a religious belief it ceases to be bigamy; it is polygamy, or "a plurality of wives," for not even the Mormons have advocated polyandry, or a plurality of husbands. Bigamy, according to their notion, is a crime against good morals, but a plurality of wives is a religious rite, or duty, sanctioned by the usage of the patriarchs, and expressly authorized by a divine revelation to the founders of the Church of the Latter Day Saints. They pretend to advocate a large liberty in the matter of plural marriages, leaving individual Mormons to choose for themselves whether they shall have one, two, or more wives. The divine law relating to polygamy is permissive, not mandatory. But it is notorious that a non-polygamous Mormon is regarded with distrust and suspicion. If the right to engage in plural marriages was of sufficient moment to justify a special revelation from heaven, they argue, it is in the nature of a divine ordinance which cannot be lightly neglected. Being a divinely-revealed ordinance, its observance has become incorporated into the religious faith and practice of the Mormon Church. It is lawful, they urge, to marry several wives, because the law of God, which is higher than human statutes, has authorized it. To enact a statute forbidding plural marriages is to infringe the clause of the Constitution forbidding legislation which "prohibits the free exercise of religion." Similarly, a sect which should pretend, or believe, that incest, infanticide, or murder was a divinely appointed ordinance to be observed under certain conditions, could set up that the enforcement of the common law, as against either of these practices, was an invasion of the rights of conscience.

The courts, however, have made short work of George Reynolds and his celebrated test case. The decision of the United States Supreme Court, though it has been anticipated, will carry dismay into many Mormon families. To be sure, the conviction of bigamous Mormons is yet encompassed with many difficulties. The necessity of obtaining non-Mormon jurors, and the difficulty of securing evidence of guilt from the homes of those who are most interested in perpetuating this last of "the twin relics of barbarism," will continue to operate against future convictions. But a great gain has been secured in the organized effort to crush out polygamy in Utah. There is now an unbroken line of the highest precedents in favor of the constitutionality of the law of 1862. The highest tribunal in the Republic has decided that bigamy committed in any Territory of the United States is an indictable offense, and punishable by fine and imprisonment. Ways and means for procuring convictions may be found and, whether Mormonism will be seriously affected by the destruction of polygamy or not, this degrading practice cannot be very long-lived.

Aiming at Religion.

BY THE NEW YORK TIMES | SEPT. 12, 1881

A go-as-you-please Sunday wanted by residents of Newark.

AT A MEETING of the Citizens' Protective Association, held yesterday afternoon at the Academy of Music, Newark, the committee of citizens appointed at a public meeting last Sunday presented a preamble and set of resolutions which were adopted by the society and will be presented to the Constitutional Commission for consideration. The preamble recites various sections in the Constitution of the United States and of several States relating to religious liberty and the observance of the Sabbath. The resolutions, among other things, say: "The preservation of a weekly civil day of rest is acknowledged as desirable by all, but in our opinion public order, morality, and religion would be far better advanced if the narrow restrictive features of the present statutes were abrogated, and thousands upon thousands of good, true, honest, sober, and industrious citizens would be no longer forced in their rights to the enjoyment of life and the pursuit of happiness to either become open violators of a law which has long been a dead letter or be hypocrites. We therefore request you to entertain the proposition of the following amendment to the Constitution:

> No law shall be passed, nor shall any existing law remain in force, which deprives any citizen of this State of the right of full enjoyment of life and happiness according to the dictates of his own conscience, so long as in such enjoyment or pursuit he does not conflict with the right of others.
>
> We would further memorialize your honorable commission regarding another point of constitutional amendment, the propriety of which will be sufficiently apparent by comparing article I., section 3 of the Constitution with the act concerning taxation, section 62. In the first we read: 'Nor shall any person be obliged to pay tithes, taxes or other rates for building any church or churches, place or places of worship, or for the maintenance of any minister or ministry, contrary to what he believes

to be right or has deliberately and voluntarily engaged to perform.' And the act concerning taxes says: 'The following persons and property shall be exempt from taxation, viz., all colleges, academies, or seminaries of learning, public libraries and school-houses, and all buildings erected and used for religious worship, the lands whereon the same are erected, the furniture thereof, and the personal property thereon.'

This exemption of so-called church property from taxation is, if not in letter, certainly in spirit, a violation of the Constitution. The amount of additional tax which would accrue if such exemption did not exist must be made up by taxing other property, and the citizens generally are, therefore, made, willing or not, in an indirect way, to pay taxes for churches, just what section 3, article I. of the Constitution especially prohibits. In view of the constantly increasing wealth and value of religious corporations and increasing burdens upon the general tax-payer, nothing appears more just than that this incongruity of statute law to the Constitution should be removed. We beg leave, therefore, to lay before your commission the following amendment to the Constitution:

Neither the State nor any municipal corporation shall exempt from taxation the property of any church or religious corporation of whatever denomination.

Sunday Under the Penal Code.

BY THE NEW YORK TIMES | DEC. 3, 1882

WHOEVER UNDERTAKES TO revise the laws suffers the discomfort that if he puts forth any improvements he is told he ought to have stated the laws exactly as they stood, but if he prints objectionable laws without changes he is reproached for all their defects. The draftsmen of the Penal Code are not exempt. There is an outburst of complaint because they have restated Sunday laws which have for years stood in force on the older statute-books of the State, though seldom regarded or enforced. The friends of a strict Sabbath observance are delighted over the apparent revival of ideas they have long striven to resuscitate. Lovers of liberty are appalled at the seeming reenactment of "blue laws." Policemen and inferior magistrates are bestirring themselves to learn what new duties the new law imposes. But we believe that all serious difficulty will be removed when the questions now rife are brought before the Judges of the higher courts for explanation. A code sometimes suffers, indeed, from a disposition on the part of case-bound Judges to construe it in a way to render it unpopular and secure its repeal; but if the Sunday chapter in the Penal Code can have a candid interpretation, it will not be found harsh.

Disregarding a few sections defining the "day" as running from midnight to midnight, protecting seventh-day Christians in their peculiar observance, &c., the Sunday law is comprised in ten sections. The first states the ground and reason of Sunday legislation. It will be remembered that many of the prohibitions were enacted half and even three-quarters of a century ago, when the idea had not been fully abandoned that the State might enforce religious duties. The modern notion is that Sunday laws can go no further than to protect the quiet of those who wish to enjoy the day religiously. The codifiers were not at liberty to change the laws, but they have declared their purpose in a way which sets a limit on their enforcement. The declaration is:

SEC. *259. The first day of the week being by general consent set apart for rest and religious uses, the law prohibits the doing on that day of certain acts hereinafter specified, which are serious interruptions of the repose and religious liberty of the community.*

This is immediately followed by:

SEC. *260. A violation of the foregoing prohibition is Sabbath-breaking.*

Then comes a list of the "acts specified" as follows:

SEC. *262. The following acts, as explained in the next six sections, are those forbidden to be done on the first day of the week, except in a work of necessity or charity: 1. Servile labor; 2. Public sports and shows: 3. Trades, manufactures, or mechanical employments; 4. Public traffic; 5. Serving process.*

Then come five sections which embody the old prohibitions upon these five-branches or kinds of conduct. To these one may look to learn what is meant by "public sports" and "traffic," but neither of them authorizes any punishment. Lastly is a section fixing the punishment of "Sabbath-breaking" at a fine of not less than $1 nor more than $10 or imprisonment for not more than ten days, or both. But this punishment is not authorized for all forms of prohibited conduct. It is imposed only for "Sabbath-breaking," and is limited by section 259 to acts which are serious interruptions of the repose and religious liberty of the community. The reason of the entire body of these laws being thus authoritatively declared, will it not be the duty of the courts to apply the maxim that "when the reason ceases the law ceases," and to restrain prosecutions to those forms of Sunday activity which are "serious interruptions."

To illustrate by a supposed case: A barber who opens his shop and shaves customers will perhaps be arrested. The complainants will cite the prohibitions on servile labor or on trades; but these are prohibitions merely; they do not authorize any punishment or even an arrest. The argument for the barber will be that his trade — considering its nature, usefulness, and usual incidents — cannot be deemed a serious interruption of the repose and religious liberty of the community. Must not this question be decided against him before the courts can fine or imprison him for Sabbath-breaking? We do not mean that the individual can defend himself in the plea that his particular shop is quietly conducted; such a doctrine would lead to insufferable favoritism. But can he not challenge his prosecutors to show that his trade as usually conducted interrupts repose and religious liberty? In nearly all prosecutions under the Sunday laws in the Penal Code this would seem to be a legitimate question, one for the Police and magistracy in the first place, for the superior courts afterward. And unless a form of labor, amusement, or business can be pronounced an interruption of the general repose and religious liberty, it will not be easy to find authority in the Code for punishing it.

Thus understood, the Code may be harmonized with the progress of American law. Throughout the land former traces of a religious purpose in these laws have disappeared. The first day of the week is named as the legal rest-day because it is generally observed, not because law undertakes to enforce any supposed Divine command. The purpose of such laws is the protection of the liberty of the masses for rest and worship. And protecting church service is not a chief element; the theory is not that some favored persons wish to attend church, but that the community has a need that the masses should have a day of rest; a stated day during which needless demands of business, attractions of demoralizing or doubtful amusements, and the noise and tumult of every-day life shall not be suffered to hinder those from resting who need repose, those from worshiping who wish to worship. All tastes having been considered, the State declares that, for the general comfort, "six days shall be free for the pursuit of labor, business, and pleasure; and the quiet people must bear with the excitement and activity. One day shall be protected for quiet and repose, and the active classes must submit to moderate restrictions." The Judges need not find it difficult to administer the Penal Code in this spirit.

Sabbath a Day of Rest

BY THE NEW YORK TIMES | DEC. 27, 1896

JUSTICE PRYOR, in the Supreme Court, yesterday, denied the application of the "Agudath Hakehiloth of New York," for a certificate of incorporation, and in refusing the certificate delivered an opinion which treats of the American Sabbath.

According to the petition of the association, the objects for which the corporation was to be formed are, "to promote the strict observance of and adherence to such customs, laws, usages, and rites of the Orthodox Hebrew religion, or faith, as are not repugnant to, and inconsistent with, the Constitution and laws of the United States and the laws of the State of New York; to improve the condition of the Orthodox Hebrew congregations, and to abolish the now existing religious evils."

The clause in the petition to which Judge Pryor excepts is this one:

"The time of holding its annual meeting is to be on each and every second Sunday of January of each and every year."

In refusing the certificate Justice Pryor says:

> In the certificate submitted to me I observe that the annual meeting of the proposed corporation is appointed to be held 'on each and every second Sunday of January of each and every year.' It is not a religious corporation, and its annual meetings are for the performance of precisely such secular business as is transacted by other civil corporations.
>
> The question is not whether such meetings on Sunday are illegal, but whether they should be approved by a Justice of the Supreme Court. A thing may be lawful and yet not laudable.

SABBATH PROTECTED BY COMMON LAW.

> 'In the State of New York the Sabbath exists as a day of rest by the common law, and without the necessity of legislative action to establish it, and may be protected from desecration by such laws as the Legislature,

in its wisdom, may deem necessary to secure to the community the privilege of undisturbed worship and to the day itself that outward respect
and observance which may be deemed essential to the peace and good
order of society, and to preserve religion and its ordinances from open
reviling and contempt.' (Lindenmuller vs. The People, 33 Barb., 548.)
'The Christian Sabbath is one of the civil institutions of the State, and
the Legislature, for the purpose of promoting the moral and physical
well being of the people and the peace, quiet, and good order of society,
has authority to regulate its observance and prevent its desecration.'
(People vs. Moses, 140 N. Y., 215.) This sanctity of the Christian Sabbath
is sanctioned and secured by repeated acts of legislation extending from
the colonial period to the present year, and as well by the impressive
deliverances of the Court of Appeals. As Justice of the Supreme Court, I
may not approve that which the immemorial and uniform policy of the
State condemns.

AGGRESSION UPON CHRISTIAN SABBATH.

Although not explicitly stated, it is nevertheless an inference, from the
face of the certificate before me, that the members of the proposed corporation are of a race and religion by which not the first but the seventh
day of the week is set apart for religious observance. The fact might be of
decisive importance were a desecration of their holy day contemplated;
but the act intended is an aggression upon the Christian Sabbath. The
law, which scrupulously protects them in the observance of their ceremonial, gives them no license, and I am sure they have no desire to affront
the religious susceptibilities of others. True, to a prosecution for work
or labor on the first day of the week, the defendant may plead that 'he
uniformly keeps another day of the week as holy time and does not labor
on that day, and that the labor complained of was done in such manner
as not to interrupt or disturb other persons in observing the first day
of the week as holy time.' (Penal Code, Section 264); but otherwise the
legislation of the State against profanation of the Christian Sabbath is
operative and imperative upon all classes of the community.

Because the holding of corporate meetings on Sunday is contrary to
the public policy of the State, if not to the letter of its law, I decline to
approve this certificate.

Application refused.

The names of the Directors of the proposed association are Moses Singer, 426 Grand Street; Samuel Fried, 328 East Fourth Street; Leopold Weizenhoffer, 334 East Houston Street, and Aaron Weisberger, 319 East Fourth Street.

A BURST OF INDIGNATION.

Reporters for The New York Times saw a number of prominent Jewish rabbis and lawyers yesterday and asked their opinions on the decision of Justice Pryor. All were emphatic in their views that the Justice had strained the interpretation of the State law. Their views follow:

The Rev. Dr. Gustave Gottheil of Temple Emanu-El, 521 Fifth Avenue, said:

> *A decision of a Supreme Court Justice ought always to be treated with becoming respect, otherwise I would not consider the decision worthy of serious criticism. It is certainly an extraordinary attempt to protect the rights of the church by the direct encroachment on the rights of another, and, worse than this, it is a return to the mediaeval principle, which we have happily outgrown, to make the courts of justice the guardians of religious institutions. It is admitted that the association which seek the right of incorporation is a purely religious one, and how one annual meeting of such a society can in any way interfere with the due observance by other people of that day as a day of rest is very difficult to see.*

DR. GOTTHEIL SARCASTIC.

> *The Judge may be assured that there is no danger of its members getting drunk or disorderly at their meetings. Neither will their singing of hymns or less objectionable songs be so loud and boisterous as to disturb their Christian neighbors. It could hardly be believed, if we had been told so, that religion could be construed by a Judge of an American court as seemingly to extend its application to the Christian Church alone. I hope that in the interest of peace and good will among the various denominations the decision will not stand.*

A HEBREW LAWYER'S POINTS.

Ex-Judge M. S. Isaacs had the following statement to make:

Mr. Justice Pryor is usually so punctilious and accurate that it is to be regretted that in this opinion he has gone just a little too far. While he may be technically correct in refusing his approval to the certificate in question, (for fixing the day of its annual meeting is not a legitimate part of a certificate of incorporation,) he is in error in holding that a corporation cannot meet on Sunday. Many charitable corporations in this State habitually meet on Sunday, and their principal business is necessarily transacted on the only day of the week which permits their officers to come together for consultation.

The Judge's contention might apply with equal force to the publication by well-known corporations of the Sunday edition of newspapers. Besides, there is grave doubt whether the authorities quoted wholly support the contention as to the sanctity of the Christian Sabbath. The Sunday laws are substantially police regulations to secure rest and quiet for citizens who 'observe Sunday as holy time.' The exception as to works of necessity and charity would probably cover such meetings of a benevolent corporation, as, under the decision of our courts, they excuse what formerly were considered infractions of the Sunday law.

DR. KOHLER WARMLY DISSENTS.

The Rev. Dr. K. Kohler of Congregation Beth-El, Fifth Avenue and Seventy-sixth Street, said:

All our charitable and religious institutions, without exception, have meetings on Sunday, and we would advise Judge Pryor to close them all. The decision will not stand. It seems to me that it is the best thing people can do on Sunday, when they hold meetings of that sort. In itself the question of enforcing the Sunday law upon those who keep Saturday as their Sabbath, like the Jews and Seventh Day Adventists and Baptists, is not legal. It might be legal in Russia, but not here. Even some church institutions hold their meetings on Sunday, for that is the day a man is free from other business cares and toil, and can devote time, mind, and heart to things of a higher religious or philanthropic purpose. The decision is unreasonable, and I have little doubt but what it will be overruled. I sincerely hope that the association will not yield, but will appeal for the sake of the principle of non-interference in matters of conscience and personal liberty, upon which this decision encroaches. I also hope that it will meet with the support of all the Jews.

THE JUDGE'S ARGUMENT A QUIBBLE.

The Rev. Stephen S. Wise of the Madison Avenue Congregation, said:

It seems to me the argument of Justice Pryor is merely a quibble. He allows that the Jews observe the Biblical seventh day as their Sabbath. That being true, there is no alternative left them but the transaction of such nominal business as presents itself in the course of congregational life, upon that day of the week, which is legally, not religiously, a day of cessation of labor. Were Judge Pryor's decision, if decision that may be called, which, in his own words, is simply the personal expression of an unauthoritative opinion, to be retroactive in effect, it would simply efface by one fell stroke practically all Jewish congregations now existing. If I may be permitted to dissent from the opinion of the distinguished jurist, I would say that the institution for whose existence a certificate of incorporation was solicited, is distinctly a religious corporation.

Technically, the business which it might transact at its annual meeting might be designated as business, but it is certainly correct to interpose that any business transacted by a body of men gathered according to corporate title for the purpose of religious worship partakes so largely of a religious character that the appellation, if not unjust, is none the less misleading. The transactions carried on by a religious corporation can at best but be incidental to the other more important matters for which it is primarily called into existence.

I believe that Judge Pryor's decision will not stand the test or scrutiny of a higher tribunal, but that the right of a Jewish religious corporation to meet on the first day Sabbath will be fully vindicated by a decision which will view the question at issue in its higher and broader bearing.

RABBI MENDES EMPHATIC.

The Rev. H. Pereira Mendes, rabbi of Shearith Israel, in West Nineteenth Street, when shown the opinion of Justice Pryor, said:

Justice Pryor considers a meeting of a Jewish society, if held on a

Sunday, improper. I fail to see the difference, however, between a Jewish society holding its annual meetings on Sunday, and providing for them in its constitution openly and publicly, and in another Jewish society which holds its meetings on a Sunday, although such meetings are not provided for in its constitution.

A large number of our greatest Jewish societies hold their meetings on Sundays. Of course, they do not disturb the public peace. I am summoned to the annual meeting of a Jewish society that will be held to-morrow. Its annual meetings have been held on Sunday for many years, as I can remember. Nobody has ever interfered. No authority has ever said it was wrong. The President of it is a man who would be the last to permit the meeting to be held on that day, if it were in any way illegal or improper.

It seems to me that if a meeting is held without disturbing the public peace and 'in such manner as not to interrupt or disturb other persons in observing the first day of the week as holy time,' no one need complain. To my mind, there is less wrong in holding a meeting on Sunday, if decorously conducted, to promote such worthy objects as are set forth in the constitution of the society in question, than to allow quasi-sacred concerts amid associations not at all conducive to Sabbath sanctity, and to making the Sabbath day 'a holy time.' A few weeks ago there was a six days' bicycle race. I am not aware that the hour or two preceding the start, which hours fell on Sunday, were much of 'a holy time.'

THE TRUE CHRISTIAN SABBATH.

But I take higher ground than Justice Pryor. If, as he says, the State legislates against the profanation of the Christian Sabbath, it becomes the duty of the State to find out which is the Christian Sabbath. The Christian Sabbath is the Sabbath that was observed by Jesus, the Founder of Christianity. He observed the seventh-day Sabbath, and the seventh-day Sabbath was observed by his followers until about the year 324, when, under the auspices of Constantine — who had turned Christian, but who was a murderer, a hypocrite, and one of the greatest villains that ever breathed — the first day of the week was exalted into the Sabbath Day.

There is not a single Christian minister who can defend that change, in view of the fact that Jesus said 'not one jot or tittle of the law' was to be changed. There is not a single 'Christian minister but knows; if he believes in Father, Son, and Holy Ghost, that by keeping Sunday as the

Sabbath he acts contrary to the spirit of the law that Jesus preached to establish, and he dishonors the Father to honor the Son; for the real reason that Sunday is observed as a sacred day is well known to be the fact that the earliest Christians met on that day in honor of their Lord, who they believed was resurrected on that day. These early Christians emphatically did not observe Sunday as the Sabbath. It was their 'Lord's Day.' They all observed the seventh day as their Sabbath.

BACK TO FIRST PRINCIPLES.

It has often seemed strange to me that the Protestants, whose object has always been to get back to first principles and to reject all human accretions on their faith, should not go back to first principles as the founder of the faith established them. Among these first principles is the consecration of the seventh day as the Sabbath. Would that at some synod of Presbyterians, Episcopalians, Methodists, or Baptists — or at some Lambeth Council — some Christian prelate could, have the courage to make a stand for a true Sabbath day!

The face of their Christ is always depicted as mild and ideal, but I fancy that face would be lighted up by a flash of anger and indignation, its lips would curl in contempt, its eyes would tell of condemnation, if He should come to earth now and see how His followers outrage and insult His honor by setting aside the commands of the God whom He worshipped, and whom He wished every one to call 'Father.' I can imagine Him furiously denouncing such splitting of hairs and such forcing of camels through the eyes of needles as have been done by Christian Pharisees. I can imagine Him urging His priests to honor the God whom He honored by honoring His commands, and among them the one that says: 'Remember the Sabbath day to keep it holy; the seventh day is the Sabbath of the Lord'; and on these conferences and synods refusing, I can imagine Him wringing His hands in despair and crying out, 'Father, forgive them, for they know not what they do.'

If this country is a Christian country, and Justice Pryor is a Christian, the law that Christ preached and practiced should be observed, and should overrule State law. The logical solution is that Hebrews should be allowed to meet on Sunday, and that the Christian Sabbath should be transferred to the seventh day.

If Christ came to New York, then, to be consistent with His own teachings, He would have to attend a Jewish synagogue for Sabbath worship. It is absurd to think that He would give Himself the lie.

PRAISE FOR CHRISTIANITY.

I am one of those Hebrews who recognize the magnificent and beautiful work accomplished in the world by Christianity. It elevated all the pagan races of Europe from Olympus to Calvary. It has strewn the world with flowers of wondrous beauty. Let it now lift the world still higher, from Calvary to Sinai, and do what that race is doing, even the race in which their Christ was born 'to blossom and bud, and fill the face of the world with fruit.'

Now what Christian minister has the courage to make the first move. He would be a Christian, a follower of his Christ's example, and not a Christian, certainly not a Constantinian Christian.

SIMON STERNE CALMLY CRITICAL.

Simon Sterne said:

I think that Justice Pryor has certainly strained a point in making his decision. The Jewish society in question is an organization of a wholly non-business character, and it looks like straining matters very greatly to declare that it would be against public policy to allow it to hold its annual meetings on Sunday. A great many of the Hebrew societies hold their elections on Sunday, and very naturally, because it is an enforced holiday, and they have time to attend to such duties on that day. In the case of hospitals and charitable institutions, I feel quite certain that most of them elect their officers on Sunday. At their meetings on Sunday, besides the elections, reports are read or submitted.

It seems a little captious in Judge Pryor, who is a learned and liberal man, and who is no Puritan. I do not suppose for an instant that he would refuse to hold as valid the election of any of these officers who had been chosen on Sunday. Many of them are among our best citizens, and some are prominent and able lawyers.

It is one thing to prevent labor that would destroy Sunday as a day of rest, and quite a different thing to prevent a semi-religious organization from choosing its officers on Sunday. The latter would not interfere in the slightest degree with any one in the strictest observance of the day. This restraint is not put upon Hebrews in England. They meet there on Sunday without restriction.

I am sorry that the decision of Justice Pryor is made in a case where it might be supposed to indicate some feeling against the Hebrews as a race and as antagonistic to the Hebrew religious faith.

Senate on Sunday Laws

BY THE NEW YORK TIMES | FEB 1, 1899

ALBANY, JAN. 31. — Excise legislation occupied the attention of the Senate to-day. Two proposed amendments to the Raines liquor tax law were presented, one by Senator Raines, raising the limit of the license fee in towns from $100 to $200, and the other by Senator Mackey, permitting the sale of liquors in cities on Sunday between the hours of 2 and 11 o'clock P. M.

In presenting his bill, Senator Mackey requested that it be referred to the Cities Committee, rather than to the Committee on Taxation and Retrenchment, by which proposed amendments to the liquor tax law heretofore have been considered. This brought forth a protest from Senator Raines, and in explanation of his request Senator Mackey said that in looking over the make-up of the committees he had concluded that the Committee on Cities would give the bill more liberal consideration than the Committee on Taxation and Retrenchment.

Senator Grady declared that the Committee on Taxation and Retrenchment was hide-bound in its opposition to any amendment to the Raines law. He warned Senator Mackey, however, that it did not make much difference to what committee the proposed amendment was referred. This Legislature had its face set against any sort of justice or fairness to the cities of the State. The Republican party must rely upon that part of the community from which it received its support because of the money of which the cities were robbed. The only legislation that would be permitted as an amendment to the Raines law would be that which the author of the law had had in incubation for some time, which would prohibit a man from drinking a glass of liquor or of spring water with his meals on Sunday.

Senator Stranahan protested against the declaration that the Republican Party was robbing the cities of the State for the benefit of the rural districts. He said that if Senator Grady meant to say that the Republican Party was arrayed upon the side of decency as against rum, he pleaded guilty, and he asserted that the Republican Party was proud of its record in this respect.

Senator Grady retorted that the rum question had never been a political one, and that there was as much affection for rum among Republicans as among Democrats.

Senator Raines then attacked the proposed amendment providing for the opening of the saloons on Sunday and said that it was the first time so bald-faced a proposition had ever been made, standing alone by itself. Attempts to attain this end had been made under different subterfuges, but he was surprised that the first proposition in so bold a form should come from a representative of the City of Buffalo. Senator Raines criticised Bishop Potter for his assertion that the saloon was the poor man's club. He said he would like to have that New York Bishop go to the tenement houses and see the conditions which existed there because of these poor men's clubs.

Senator Foley spoke in defense of the proposition to open the saloons on Sunday afternoons. He did not know by what right Senator Raines assumed to represent the morality of the State. He asserted that the Raines law hotels did more for the degradation of the community than all the poor men's clubs.

The debate drifted into a political discussion, and Senator Mackey made an extended speech, replying to Senator Raines, in which he asserted that the sentiment of the people of Buffalo was in favor of this amendment. It was the issue upon which the last election was contested, and it was the issue responsible for the Democratic victory there.

Senator Raines made an extended speech in general defense of the liquor tax law. He declared that the provision permitting the sale of liquor in hotels on Sunday had existed in the old law, and it had then been used by Tammany Hall as a club to extort tribute from saloon keepers.

Senator Grady replied that whenever Senator Raines found himself short of argument he resorted to hurling anathemas at Tammany Hall. He asserted that there was not a man in the Tammany organization who did not stand as well in public estimation as did Senator Raines. It might do for some hayseed to talk such ridiculous nonsense about Tammany Hall, but Senator Raines came from the seclusion of Ontario County often enough to know better.

The discussion having continued for nearly two and a half hours, the objection to the reference of the bill to the Committee on Taxation and Retrenchment was withdrawn and it was so referred.

In addition to his proposed amendment to the liquor tax law, Senator Mackey introduced five bills providing for greater liberality in the observance of Sunday than is permitted by existing laws. He proposes to add to the works of necessity and charity, which are now permitted, any labor essential to recreation or convenience. One of his bills permits the delivery as well as the sale of food before 12 o'clock, and provides that ices, ice cream, mineral water, nuts, magazines, books, periodicals, and other publications, and furnishing goods may be sold in a quiet and orderly manner at any time of the day.

Another bill permits shooting, hunting, fishing, playing horse racing, or other public sports, exercises, or shows which shall not seriously interfere with and interrupt the repose and religious liberty of the community on Sunday. Another amends the Penal Code so that trades, manufactures, agricultural, or mechanical employments may be carried on Sunday when they are works of necessity, and when they carried on in such a way as not to interfere with the general repose of the community.

Sunday Closing Campaign

BY THE NEW YORK TIMES | FEB. 13, 1899

THE CAMPAIGN STARTED by the West Side Sunday Closing Association to compel the delicatessen, grocery, and other stores to close at 10 o'clock on Sunday mornings was carried on with vigor yesterday, notwithstanding the inclement weather, by members of the association who had volunteered to act as watchers. Their efforts were seconded by the police, who closed all delicatessen stores found open after the hour named, or, rather, all but one. Abraham P. Krakaur, who keeps a store at 590 Columbus Avenue, refused to obey the orders of the police and was arrested. This was the only arrest made. He was taken to the police station in West One Hundredth Street and released on bail. He returned straight to his store, which he kept open from 4 to 7 P. M., as it has been his custom to do, and despite the fact that the previous Sunday he had been arrested three times.

"We shall continue to keep open Sundays as usual from 7 to 12 o'clock in the morning and from 4 to 7 in the evening, and the police and blue-law cranks can't prevent us," said Mrs. Krakaur last evening.

Police Captain Haughey of this precinct means well. He thinks he is doing his duty, but he doesn't know the law about it. We do, and my husband, acting for himself and in the interest of the Delicatessen Dealers' Association, is going to make another test case.

I say another test case, for this isn't the first time we've been persecuted. Five years ago this matter was thrashed out, with the result that the case against us was dismissed. Several other cases of a similar character have also been dismissed. We sell nothing but cooked food, and cannot be regarded otherwise than as caterers. Caterers, like the cigar and drug stores, have a right to do business on Sundays.

NECESSARY TO KEEP OPEN.

The fact is people couldn't very well get on without us. The New York Times in its editorial on Wednesday last exactly described the situation when it said that everybody that lives in New York knows that it is the custom of nine-tenths of the householders to give their servants Sunday evening off and to get their meals from delicatessen stores and restaurants. Why, as is observed, should not the 'ancient and fishlike statute,' which prevents the selling of the necessaries of life, and 'which has been perverted into an instrument of blackmail and persecution, be modified to suit the habits of a community of three millions of people?' It couldn't have been better put, and we pasted the article in our store window so that the people in the quarter could read and take it to heart.

A proof of the correctness of its statements is that we receive from 100 to 150 orders to furnish meals every Sunday, without counting the purchases made by people who take the food away with them. This shows you that the delicatessen stores are a necessity and are bound to keep open on Sundays. No attempt to close them has been made outside of this precinct.

A tradesman on Amsterdam Avenue was indignant at the action of the association, although being a dealer in cigars and tobacco his business was not affected by it.

"It's absurd," he exclaimed. "A pretty spectacle we present to Europeans, trying to impose blue laws in the leading American city upon millions of the most progressive people in the world. To be logical these church people would have to prevent cars from running, and churches from opening, and shut off every kind of employment on Sundays."

WILL HAVE LAWS ENFORCED.

Edward L. Gridley, President of the West Side Sunday Closing Association, frankly admitted that the tradesman's argument was right. "But we cannot change the laws," he went on,

though we can and propose to see to it that those existent are enforced. The association was founded last winter, but it is only just settling down to work. It originated in this way: A woman member of St. Michael's

Chapter of C. A. I. L., had her attention called to the fact that a Sunday school boy employed in a fish market was unable to attend morning church or Sunday school. Reporting the fact to the chapter, a committee of investigation was formed.

This committee, discovering that a want of consideration for Sunday was not confined to non-church members, but that many church people ordered goods on that day, felt that help must be sought from the churches in the immediate neighborhood, and about a year ago appealed to all the clergymen in the vicinity. Dr. Shaw of the West End Presbyterian Church cordially responded, and immediately appointed a committee from his church. Soon after the West Side Sunday Closing Association was formed, consisting of committees from St. Michael's, West End Presbyterian, Grace Methodist Episcopal, and Park Presbyterian Churches.

This morning the volunteer detectives were out all over the neighborhood. When we discover that the law is being infringed we report the offenders to the police. I myself noted three instances on Columbus Avenue this morning. I saw a coal dealer sell coal to a woman and a grocer sell a can of kerosene to another woman. A hardware store also admitted customers when they knocked. We feel that we have right and the public on our side, and shall go ahead. That is why we issued lists of the tradesmen who were conforming to and disobeying the law. The West Side Grocers' Association has promised to co-operate with us by adhering strictly to the letter of the law.

Five cabinet workers and a varnisher, who were at work on a new building on the Boulevard last Sunday, were arrested on complaint of a walking delegate of the Cabinetmakers' Association. It was said that the association was co-operating with us. So it was, but not to our knowledge. We do not even know the delegate. But the incident shows that the workingmen themselves are in favor of Sunday rest, and we hope to secure the support of the labor unions.

A DAY OF REST NEEDED.

The Rev. Dr. Philip M. Watters, pastor of Grace Methodist Episcopal Church, who has taken an active part in the Sunday closing movement, explained its purport yesterday.

I think The New York Times, although its impartiality is proverbial, has taken a rather one-sided view of the matter," said he.

It doubtless was not fully informed as to our aims and views. This is no fanatical, religious movement, although, of course, we use the influence of the churches to further it, because we are satisfied that the cause is a good one. We are seeking to enforce a day of rest not upon religious grounds, but because a day of rest is a social necessity. So widely is this recognized that the German Socialists, who I imagine will hardly be suspected of religious leanings, have introduced a bill in the Reichstag to enforce a weekly day of rest.

It is absolutely essential that the workingman should have a chance for recreation and to see his family one day out of the seven. We are tending more and more toward the undesirable European Sabbath, which is anything but a day of rest for a large portion of the community, and we need to combine and stand up for the maintenance of our ancient privileges on this day for the benefit of the people.

We would like to see all the stores close for the whole day on Sunday. Butchers' clerks and others with whom I have talked are grateful for the efforts we are making on their behalf. 'We have to work until 12 o'clock Saturday nights,' they say, 'and we would be happy, indeed, if we could get a whole day off, like other employees.' Personally I have found little opposition to the movement from the storekeepers themselves. They say they have no objection to close if others in the same line of business will agree to do the same. Individually they are afraid to close because they run the risk of losing their customers, who naturally would go elsewhere. I quite appreciate their position, and we are trying to remedy this by getting all of them to discontinue business on Sunday.

CHURCH PEOPLE TO CONFER.

There is no real necessity for keeping open. There are few really poor people in this section, which is inhabited for the most part by thrifty middle-class families who could easily make provision for a closed day. It seems to me that it is carelessness, a lack of forethought that is leading to this increasing laxity of the observance of the Sabbath.

A conference of delegates from all the churches in this section will be held in the parish house of St. Michael's Episcopal Church on Feb. 21 to devise means of impressing the matter forcibly upon the public, and for securing general co-operation in the work of obtaining for working men and women a much needed day of rest.

In St. Michael's Church Dr. Peters prefaced his sermon by saying that he wished to explain a few points regarding the movement. The movement was instituted for a twofold reason — that of inducing people to properly observe the Sabbath from a sense of religious duty, and the sentiment which prompts the Church people to have a regard for the comfort of the individuals who are compelled to work on the day which should be set apart for rest.

The notice sent out last week by Capt. Chapman of the Eldridge Street Police Station through his detectives that he intended to enforce the Sunday law relating to tradesmen, saloon keepers, and barbers had its effect, and the blotter at nightfall showed a sum total of but two arrests.

Early in the day Capt. Chapman sent out several detectives in plain clothes. Shortly after 2 o'clock an innocent looking man went into Israel Grossman's clothing store, at 51 Hester Street. The day being blustery, Israel recommended everything from a pair of socks to a storm overcoat. The purchase of a pair of gloves led to his arrest. The innocent-looking man in plain clothes was Detective Sheehan. David Kingsley of 20 Ludlow Street, in the same line of business, came to brief at the hands of Detective Lewis.

The barbers' shops were all apparently closed, and many a late Sunday riser who had been in the habit of getting a surreptitious shave found himself compelled to go without or travel to another precinct. Capt. Chapman himself made a tour of the precinct during the afternoon, and returned to the station house satisfied that his orders had been generally obeyed. "The precinct is shut up tightly," commented the Captain.

New York City and the Ironclad Sunday Law

BY J. I. C. CLARKE | DEC. 8, 1907

ATROCIOUS! WAS EX-JUDGE Dittenhoefer's characterization of the Sunday law as laid down by Justice James A. O'Gorman in his recent and sweeping decision.

And yet it has practically been the law since New York became a State, and was the common law in the century before. Judge O'Gorman did not make it. He does not come of the race or faith that looks with an unkindly eye on all Sunday amusements, particularly such as tend to the joy of life and can be had without hurt to the moral law. But a Judge has to interpret statutes in the light of their enactment, and the law against "Sabbath-breaking" is as ironclad as the helmet of a Roundhead; it is Puritan law in all its sternness. If John Alden with Priscilla on his arm were to meet Miles Standish to-night in the neighborhood of Times Square, the stalwart Miles could look with a warrior smile at the closed doors of the theatres and the three feel as much at home as "In the Old Colony days in Plymouth, the land of the Pilgrims."

Down past the Broadway Theatre and the Metropolitan Opera House silence and darkness; down past the Empire and the Knickerbocker darkness and silence. Up by the Criterion and the New York, across by the Astor, dumbness and dusk; westward, by the Belasco, the New Amsterdam, the Lyric, the Liberty, the Hackett, the American, mirk and hush; and, oh! on the northwest corner of Forty-second Street and Seventh Avenue deepest shade and profoundest depths of taciturnity enshrouding Hammerstein's Victoria! There may be crowds of the curious or the indignant patrolling the neighborhood, just as people go out of their way to pass by some commonplace house where recent murder has been done; but they will neither be flocking to the theatres nor pouring out of them. The ancient grip of the Reverend Nicholas Bound is upon New York State and City as firmly as he would have it when he wrote his famous plea for the Puritan Sunday what time Queen Elizabeth ruled manfully in England.

"All performances in theatres or other places of public amusement and entertainment on Sunday are prohibited."

BACK TO THE REV. NICHOLAS BOUND.

So says Judge O'Gorman, so said the Rev. Nicholas Bound. No beating about the bush, no trimming of the skirts of a statutory condition that only looks to labors of "necessity and charity" as the exceptions to a rigid surrender of the day to "rest and religious uses," which makes formidable lists of things that may not be done "which are serious interruptions of the repose and religious liberty of the community." It indeed makes exception — a great concession — to "whatever may be needful during the day for the good order, health, or comfort of the community." But not in these things are included any "interlude, tragedy, comedy, opera, ballet, play, farce, negro minstrelsy, negro or other dancing, or any other entertainment of the stage or any parts therein, or any equestrian circus, or dramatic performance, or any performance of jugglers, acrobats, or rope dancing." All these are forbidden, the good, the bad, the harmless, the harmful — all cut off at one swoop, like Macduff's children. Not even concerts? Their omission from the specially named forbidden things seemed, in the first stages of the examination that led up to the decision, to be held as permissible because so omitted. The decision shuts them off as effectually as a "turn" by the "Great Aerial Knockabout Three." In Judge O'Gorman's construction of the law he finds ample support for his view. The law is ironclad. Custom, public tendency, official complacency have set up another standard. Sunday concerts, when permitted at all as "sacred concerts," have been taken as license for vaudeville, even for plays in foreign languages, and all the while the grim old law was sleeping with all its iron teeth in its gums, waiting for the hand of religious zealotry to get it out of its ancient truckle bed and plump it with a rattling of bones before the Supreme Court, where the Judge sets it on the Great

White Way to ravage the plans of Messrs. Conried, Hammerstein, and Klaw & Erlanger.

It is the way of people who are in earnest about anything to fight for it until they get it. The first blow has fallen on some fifty managers, about a thousand performers, a like number of instrumental musicians, and some 80,000 folk of the city who were wont to pay for relaxation on Sunday afternoon or evening, the latter representing probably thrice the number of attendants at the performances who did not go to them every Sunday, what will they do about it?

Already the lawyers who represent the managers are planning ways of taking the matter to the Appellate Court, and no doubt working it up finally to the Court of Appeals. But if the law finds a strict constructionist in the Supreme Court there is little hope, it seems to an observer, of anything less drastic in the higher and drier reaches of the Temple of Law. The Court of Appeals of the State of New York, has found that a man fishing on Sunday in a brook that ran through his own farm was a Sabbath breaking misdemeanant. What hope, then, to drag even a Conried concert or a Beethoven symphony through the meshes of a law fitted with so many prohibitions?

There seems only one effective way, and that is to amend the law.

The question naturally arises, What forces will be arrayed on either side in an effort to bring the law more into consonance with the times? That cannot be answered decisively now. The power of religious sentiment is mighty, and when aroused it is apt to be ruthlessly used. It is probable that in the rural districts and villages and smaller towns of the State inflammatory appeals against "violations of the Sabbath" can be successfully made. In the larger cities other views will probably prevail because different conditions obtain. What that may mean may be surmised when already the alarm has been spread that the half million New Yorkers who visit Coney Island on Summer Sundays will, under the decision, find everything that made the great resort joyous as void and colorless as the vicinity of Times Square to-night. Now, every city and town of any considerable size throughout the State has

some equivalent of Coney Island in its vicinity to which its young and old flock for harmless diversion and a breath of fresh air on Summer Sundays. So, in that at least, there is a common cause to rally around in seeking a modern modification of the Puritan Sabbath.

APPEAL FOR AMENDMENT.

It would seem, therefore, that an appeal to the Legislature which assembles in about three weeks is the sanest course and should have some chance of success if the new provisions be limited to "cities of the first class," and no attempt be made to take in the entire State. The idea of the Christian Sabbath is deeply imbedded in the law, and the framing of amendments bristles with difficulties, but it is believed by many learned in the law that they can be surmounted if the fundamentals are not disturbed by radical innovations. How can such amendments be framed?

Before attempting to examine that point, it would be well to recall the origin of the Sabbath among the Asiatic peoples. No mistake could be greater than to think that the early Jews made a Puritan Sabbath. Rigorous as it was as to forbidding labor and enjoining rest and "holy convocation," it did not at all exclude the idea of joy and the Jewish idea of joy always included song, and doubtless dancing, as well as three good meals.

It was not, indeed, regarded Puritanically when the Sabbath was shifted from Saturday to Sunday through the first fifteen centuries of the Christian era. Nor did Martin Luther deem Sunday a day of dole. But in the ranks of those adhering to various branches of the reformed religion there arose sects whose Sunday observances became more rigid in the insistence on devotional exercises and the condemnatory exclusion of all that they accounted savoring of mundane joy. In the England of Elizabeth, James I. and Charles I. it became deeply rooted, but it was in Scotland that it attained that hold on the popular mind which has held it shut tight against any broadening to this day. In Ireland, where the laws were made by Protestants for a Catholic people, the standard of severity was also set up, but, except in the north, where Protestants still are numerous, the lightheartedness of the Celt has found a way of retaining the olden features of harmless Sunday enjoyment that do not clash with religious observances.

It is, then the Scotch-Sabbath, handed down by the Puritans of New England, which is the Sabbath of our law in the State of New York.

In considering the subject it is, however, well to remember that even a rigid Sabbath law sits less heavily on rustic than on urban human beings. In the comparative solitude of country life a hundred wants and aspirations of city folk are missing from the mental make-up. Their absence confers no superiority on the side of morals, for mostly they concern matters that are not in the domain of morals at all. The relaxation of Sunday does not bring to Reuben any awakening to the aesthetic desires that stir the man or woman of the crowded city. If it satisfies the countryman to sit on a fence on a Sunday afternoon and throw apple cores at the hens, it would be no hardship on him to be forbidden to attend a grand concert at the Manhattan Opera House in the evening.

It comes, therefore, to this, that the dweller in the city might find for himself what he wants in the way of Sunday entertainment to sweeten his rest from the work of the other six days of the week. The Londoner, slow of progress, has been waking up from his torpor on the matter of what to do with his Sunday, and has been moving forward by the process of amending the law rather than by the New York process of first evading it and then getting heated over its sudden enforcement. It is not so long ago that secular entertainments of every kind were forbidden in London on Sunday, and even yet they are limited to concerts of sober, dignified character, or to entertainments mild and parochial as to quality, yet affording pleasant evenings for the well-behaved.

When we have taken in Scotland the rigid and England the broadening, and drawn a line around New York and New England, we have pretty well bounded the territory where are legal bars against a rational enjoyment of the Sabbath on the line or modern city life. It is not such a tremendous area of the world's surface to set up against the rest of the world, is it?

It would gratify the strictest Sabbatarians to be able to say that France, which combines a great Catholic population with a very aggressive body of Atheists, was the leading "desecrator" of the Sabbath, but it is not so. Protestant Germany is just as open and broad in the matter of what may be enjoyed in the way of Sunday amusement.

WHAT PARIS DOES ON SUNDAY.

And now, if you please, let us look at Paris on a Sunday evening. The theatres are open; the circus is in full blast; the boulevards are gay with lights, and the joy of living has a hundred facets sparkling for him of Gallic mind. And is it a drunken or a shouting or a rowdy crowd? Not a bit of it. Husbands and wives and children are out together tasting the freshness of the evening. They may be seen hundreds at a time sipping sugared water at the multitude of cafés-concerts or sitting in attentive rows on the benches of the theatres, little and big. If it wounds you to see them thus merry at the theatre on Sunday, and try to tell them how much you commiserate them, what a stare of wonder you evoke! Parbleu! They and their fathers and grandfathers and — mais — long before have looked on Sunday as a pleasant day. Church in the morning, a dinner as noble as circumstances will allow, and then some amusement in the evening. Voila! And when one lives among them a little while prejudice melts away, and one realizes that state of mind at once ignorant and presumptuous which is called "insular."

In Berlin life goes easy, too, on Sunday. The grave Germans will not be denied their concerts, their plays, their operas. There, too, the day is emphatically one for the whole family, and the flocks they make in the gardens and concert halls! Soon you begin to feel that if their rational and delightful Sundays were taken from them and made close days of grimness their boasted philosophy would take an inward turn, and they would die of it. So much do they unbend, and with so much determination, that you would hesitate long before asking Hans or Gretchen to give a reason for daring to enjoy a concert stück or a play day. And they have carried this Sunday spirit wherever they have gone from the fatherland.

In Cincinnati you can see it bubbling over with a merriment borrowed from our keener air. And are they citizens either in morals or conduct that we want to be rid of or that we count as "undesirables"? Not at all, Sunday evening plays and concerts to the contrary notwithstanding. And how they love concerts, and what extraordinary combinations in the name of melody satisfy them!

In Chicago they have Sunday plays and entertainments, and no one can say that they are the worse for it. In the great Western metropolis, if anywhere, a wide-open Sunday evening would bring out the worst features; but it is susceptible of proof that the people who go to the theatre on that evening are not the lawbreakers and the rowdies, but the plain, hard-working people, who go soberly to be amused and as soberly come away. Austrians, Italians, Spaniards, when long enough in the country to understand the language, are out in force, because in their mother countries they may do the like. They have no traditions telling them to do otherwise. Many of the theatres are "dark" because the managers of the "combinations" come from the East, and the actors and actresses are not hired with a view to Sunday performances, but the majority fall in with the local habit. Reform in Chicago has many tough problems before it reaches the question of Sunday.

But what of reform in the other direction for New York? Were the tide to set so strongly here toward a broadening of Sunday customs, there should be some way of squaring the law with the fact, lest the law be a hissing in the ears of the people. So far there seems to be no popular pressure toward the opening of the theatres for regular performances on Sunday. What then shall be the limit set down?

It is only when one looks for details that the difficulty appears. Probably a consensus of public opinion would favor such concerts as are given at the two opera houses. No one who admits that would object to a symphony concert, but once you step outside that, you come into vaudeville. And what of vaudeville? In the recent examination before Judge Lawrence he found that twenty out of twenty-five "acts" cited came within his construction of the law as permissible. That portion of his decision was not allowed by Judge O'Gorman, but surely if these twenty acts were ultimately decided to be not legal, they nevertheless give us some basis for separating the vaudeville goats from the variety sheep in drawing up an amendment to the law "for cities of the first class."

QUESTION OF SUNDAY MUSIC.

But if these distinctions are made, and vocal and instrumental pieces, say, also monologues, are to be permitted, what of the quality of the songs or the talks? Who is to decide which are proper or improper on Sunday that would be tolerable the rest of the week? Truly there is no authority outside of the public attitude to the performance that would be valuable. The New York theatregoing public has been so set against impurity, week day and holiday, that moral uncleanness can be said to exist no longer on our public stage. That is not to be put to the credit of the managers, since the wisest of them only recognized the public distaste for grossness or immodesty before the footlights. It is known to all familiar with the back of the stage that the successful vaudeville managers are very prudes in their exactions that everything enacted before their audiences shall be cleanly as well as diverting. The difficulty, indeed, does not lie there. If there is an allowance of song and other music on Sunday, it ought to be general as to range and, liberal in interpretation: the audience will take care of the rest.

It is suggested that a censor might operate with advantage in such matters and settle what was and was not advisable for Sunday. Well, it is feared in some quarters that if he were a Tammany man he might favor one locality at the expense of another where "friends" most did congregate; while, if he were a Republican, he might construct a little tariff of his own that would make the days of "honest graft" look queer, but if he were the New York equivalent of a Populist he might shut up everything north of Fourteenth Street and west of the Bowery. On the whole, it is not in tone with American practice to tolerate a censor. The law should operate against offenders by information and regular process after the dereliction, not before. But a license board might deal with the general question of propriety with some show of success. In their purview it would not be the occasional slip, but the general reputation that should count.

The problem can be worked out if the limit is set where general public opinion will sustain it. That should certainly provide for reasonable latitude in the matter of local Summer resorts and for the giving of concerts.

When a law may be so construed as to stop the splendid, elevating concerts at the opera houses, the genteel performances at the Y. M. C. A., and the "lepping" and discus throwing of Sheridan at Celtic Park, in the wilds of Long Island, (although within the city limits), surely there is need for the friends of human progress to find a way of amending it to permit these things, and some others.

Dr. Wise Against Repeal of Dry Law

BY THE NEW YORK TIMES | APRIL 12, 1920

TAKING AS HIS SUBJECT "Shall Prohibition Be Repealed?" the Rev. Dr. Stephen S. Wise, in the Free Synagogue, Carnegie Hall, yesterday set forth reasons why in his opinion the Eighteenth Amendment should stand. He said there was no argument for the amendment save the threadbare, meaningless argument that personal liberty was invaded by its passage.

"It is an insult to the intelligence and dignity and honor of the American people to continue to keep the liquor issue, which has been answered, in the forefront of American life at a time when America must concern itself with momentous problems of common life that press for solution," Dr. Wise said.

On behalf of repeal it was urged that there was much dissatisfaction with prohibition and its enforcement, he said. He asked if every law was to be repealed the enforcement of which excited opposition and were the American people ready to go to the length of admitting that no law should be allowed to stand on the statute books because some people did not like it? Dr. Wise answered the argument of the "wets" that immigrants were leaving or threatening to leave a drinkless America, by putting the question of whether any American would stand up and seriously maintain that we should change American law and order to suit the personal habits and customs of a certain group of immigrants.

"That the next Presidential campaign should revolve around the issue of liquor is a disgrace to America and a calamity to its citizenship," he said.

I am against the repeal of prohibition, because the testimony of all impartial and worth-while witnesses throughout the land is to the effect that the nation has already, even within the brief period of merely partial enforcement, been greatly benefited thereby. Traveling from State to

State throughout the land, I have not heard a word in challenge of the wisdom and beneficence of the prohibition law save from the lips of a few men whose personal tastes and convivial habits are more important in their own sight than the well-being of the whole nation.

ALL ARGUMENTS STILL VALID.

I am against the repeal of the Eighteenth Amendment because every argument that was valid on behalf of prohibition continues to be valid. Alcohol has not ceased to be one of the three race poisons perpetrating its baneful effect upon the human race from generation to generation, because of the passage of the Eighteenth Amendment.

I am against the repeal of prohibition, nominal or actual, because of the character of the groups which favor repeal or annulment and the methods they are ready to employ. The criminal alliance of liquor interests and politics too long postponed the enactment of prohibition. The renewal of that criminal alliance alone can become effective in repealing prohibition. I do not believe that the American people will suffer that alliance to prevail against the will arid weal of the whole American nation.

Dr. Wise said there should be either enforcement or repeal, but not the cowardly and lawless evasion of enforcement through the outwardly lawful processes of annulment. The American people would visit its wrath upon the heads of any group or party within the nation which sought to annul the will of the people by such methods of indirection as were rife among the essentially lawless opponents of the Eighteenth Amendment, he told his congregation.

UNITARIANS EXCLUDED.

In his sermon yesterday morning the Rev. Charles Francis Potter, pastor of the West Side Unitarian Church, worshipping temporarily at Earl Hall, Columbia University, said that the campaign appeal of the Interchurch World Movement was on a Unitarian basis, but petty sectarianism had excluded the Unitarians and Universalists from participating in it. Unitarians from Channing to the present day have always been in favor of co-operative effort of Christian churches to bring the world into harmony with the spirit of Jesus, he said, but the leaders of the Interchurch Movement, holding up their puny measuring rods, had decided to exclude them.

"At the Atlantic City convention which launched this movement Professor F. D. Barton proposed that all Christian bodies be invited to co-operate," Mr. Potter said.

In response the entire audience arose to its feet. But the fact remains that in spite of that vote the Unitarians and Universalists have not been invited. The only inference is that they are not considered Christian.

Do these two groups, then, not believe in Jesus and follow him? Oh, yea. And do they not lead moral lives and are they not noted for their public spirit, generosity and philanthropy? Most certainly. What, then, is the difficulty? It seems that the two denominations do not require belief in the deity of Jesus; they conceive Him as a leader and not a god. Belief, then, in Jesus is the measuring rod of the Interchurch Movement; not the great Christian principles, but a theological dogma is made the yardstick to measure men by.

Mr. Potter said that one of the humorous facts of the campaign was that at a recent meeting of officials of the movement which he attended, they pledged themselves to try and secure religious liberty for Unitarians in Transylvania. He said that when he mildly suggested that the Unitarians in Europe might be embarrassed by having their religious liberty obtained by a group in the United States who refused to admit American Unitarians to their number because they were not Christians, he was called sectarian.

"I was informed by an official of the Interchurch Movement, not officially but privately, that Unitarians didn't amount to much anyway; they were only a handful," he said.

Is size to be the measure of importance? Less than one in a thousand in the United States are Unitarians yet in the Hall of Fame of New York University, twenty out of the fifty were members of this denomination. Yet if these twenty were alive today the only part they could take in the Interchurch Movement would be to contribute to the expenses of their own conversion to orthodoxy. There have been several Unitarians good enough to be President of the United States, but evidently they were lost souls and are now perishing in hell.

To Enforce Sunday Laws

BY THE NEW YORK TIMES | OCT. 2, 1920

PATERSON, N. J., OCT. 1. — Instructions to get evidence and to make arrests of saloonkeepers and others selling, transporting or dealing in liquor, and to make raids on any motion picture houses which may attempt to open on Sunday in violation of the Sunday laws, were contained in the monthly address this afternoon to the Police Department by Chief of Police John M. Tracey. He also instructed the police to prevent the delivery of bread on Sunday.

Chief Tracey declared that personal feeling should have nothing to do with the action of the policemen.

CHAPTER 3

Freedom for Different Groups and Sects

Certain religious groups in the United States had practices that put them at odds with the law. One of the best known is the Mormons, who practiced polygamy. They claimed it was an issue of religious freedom, but the Supreme Court disagreed, preventing Utah from becoming a state until the practice of polygamy was abolished. Other sects that faced various issues included Quakers, Jehovah's Witnesses, Christian Scientists and the Salvation Army. Conscientious objectors and those who refused to salute the flag also raised lawmakers' ire.

The Quakers on the Draft — Further Views on the Subject.

BY THE NEW YORK TIMES | AUG. 27, 1864

THE FOREIGN REVIEW contains the following loyal remarks upon the draft:

> If friends had been called upon to draw up an exemption law, it is possible they might have made it more satisfactory to themselves. They would probably prefer not being enrolled at all; yet, as the law stands, it may be regarded as simply a mode by which a certain proportion of non-combatants may be selected for peaceful duties, just as a similar proportion of other people is chosen to bear arms. Friends are enrolled

as citizens, and they are not drawn for war purposes, except so far as an indiscriminate care of the sick and wounded in military hospitals may be considered as such, and on this subject our opinions have not been withheld. Whatever views may be entertained on this point, there can be no difference of opinion in respect to the propriety of aiding in the care of the freed people.

But the principle of the question at issue does not depend upon the character of the services to which non-combatants are to be assigned. That question is, whether Friends, being released from military service, and having their claim to religious liberty and the rights of conscience fully and absolutely acknowledged by the Government, are required by their religious principles to refuse the performance of every service belonging to good citizens, under the apprehension that such performance would be an unjustifiable purchase of a religious liberty, with which Governments have no right to interfere. As well might our early Friends have refused to take the affirmation prescribed by Parliament in lieu of an oath. Oaths and bearing arms are equally prohibited in the New Testament; so that Governments have no more right to impose oath-taking than they have to require military service; and if those whose scruples against fighting procure them exemption from it, are not justifiable in yielding to the call of Government for some other service, it is clear, by parity of reason, that an affirmation cannot be taken in lieu of an oath by those who believe that swearing is not allowed under the Gospel dispensation.

Never since the Society of Friends came into existence has there been a greater necessity than at the present time for observing faithfully its testimony against bearing arms, and avoiding, as far as possible, any implication in military matters; but, in the language of a correspondent, 'it is the least of our business to study to invent crosses and sacrifices in religion.'

Friends have always believed it right to apply to Governments for relief from oppressive laws and practices; they have not sought to be martyrs, but have always gratefully accepted and acknowledged the just action of rulers and legislators in their behalf, and no mere technicality of language should induce them to refuse compliance with beneficent provisions of law on the one hand, and the just claims of their country on the other.

The Freedom of Worship Bill.

BY THE NEW YORK TIMES | FEB. 16, 1885

THE REV. DR. J. M. PULLMAN applied his discourse on "Tolerance" last evening to the pending Freedom of Worship bill. After tracing tolerance through its various stages to his present basis in reverence for liberty of conscience, he said he felt it the duty of Protestants not only to tolerate Roman Catholics, but to defend them in their rights to worship as they pleased; but when they attempted to force their methods into affairs not strictly within the church, they transcended their privileges and should be resisted. He would defend a boy in the House of Refuge against coercive proselyting on the part of Universalists as strongly as against the same thing by Roman Catholics. Liberty was the only soil on which truth could grow. So, while he would tolerate the intolerance of Romanism, yet if his Catholic neighbor tried to overstep his just privileges to gain something by fraud of force or imposition, he would resist and oppose him by every means in his power.

Dr. Pullman reviewed the work of the Catholic and Protestant Churches. The Catholic Church had started in to do the work of Christ among men, and had succeeded until corruption blocked its usefulness. The Reformation had come to break up a monopoly in God as despotic, as grasping, and as oppressive as though it enchained the very air. The world was gasping for breath when the Reformation set the free winds blowing. Belief had built cathedrals. The intellectual lines of ethics and religion along which Protestantism ran led to the conviction out of which character was built. Protestantism had not overturned one despotism to set up another. There would be no successor in that business. The world could never more be governed by the Italian method, so long as it was worth governing, and to-day energy was dying and growth had stopped wherever human infallibility was an article of faith.

This review outlined the principles which converged on the subject that is now exercising religious thought in the State. The House of Refuge had been conducted under harmonious management for 60 years. An essential feature in the management had been the firm avoidance of sectarian influences. Clergymen of any denomination were privileged to visit the chapel on Sundays, to preach Christian truths and sound morality, and Catholic priests were not shut out from participation in such exercises. They could, indeed, go further and administer the church teachings in their own way in private to such of the boys as were Catholics. No one had objected to what had been said before all. On what had been omitted there were grave differences. The result was that, by estimate, 70 per cent of the boys had been reformed through the moral and religious system of non-sectarian management. No sect had complained except the Roman Catholics, who were now clamoring for a public celebration of mass.

"It is a singular spectacle," Dr. Pullman said,

> that the Roman Catholic Union should be clamorous in New-York for freedom of worship while the head of the Catholic Church in Rome bewails the freedom of worship that allows the erection of Protestant chapels within sight of the Vatican.
>
> The Catholic Church cannot be content with toleration. Its course recalls the sway of the slave power, which was tolerated under aggression and offense until the alternative was forced upon us of lying down and submitting to it or rising and crushing it. The same aggressive spirit crops out in Utah. It can't bear toleration. So it is ever with systems that have a fatal wrong within them. They aggress and encroach until higher powers are aroused and crush them; and at no times are they so offensive as when the world is engrossed in the peaceful but busy pursuits of trade.
>
> The 'Freedom of Worship' bill should not pass because Catholics have equal privileges with other sects, and are protected in them. The mass is a purely sectarian symbol. It is not right to call on the civil power to set it up in any of our institutions. Penal and reformatory institutions are not maintained for 'freedom of worship;' not because we don't want Catholics to teach in them, but because we ought not to turn the

public institutions into propaganda for any church. Such would be a plain departure from civil and religious liberty. If any church thinks it furnishes a greater number of criminals than all the others and wants to reform them by sectarian methods, the way is plain. It must have institutions of its own. Under our Christian experience and our ideas of tolerance, a Catholic in this land can be no less than an American citizen. More than an American citizen we can never suffer him to be.

The War Upon Polygamy.

BY THE NEW YORK TIMES | OCT. 7, 1886

IN ITS ANNUAL REPORT just filed with the Secretary of the Interior the Utah Commission announces that the law disfranchising polygamists has been fully and successfully enforced. All persons practicing polygamy or unlawful cohabitation in Utah have been excluded from voting and holding office. The commission does not, however, feel certain that this penalty has had the effect of greatly diminishing the practice. There have been many prosecutions, and the penalty of fine and imprisonment has been enforced in these cases where convictions have been secured. And yet the commission says, "whether upon the whole polygamous marriages are on the decrease in Utah is a matter on which different opinions are expressed." There seems to be no doubt that in Salt Lake City many persons have been restrained by fear of disfranchisement and imprisonment from entering upon the prohibited relation, but in other parts of the Territory it is believed that violations of the law have been frequent. It is said that many polygamous marriages have taken place in the Mormon temples at Logan City and St. George, located respectively in the extreme northern and southern parts of the Territory.

It is certain that the Mormon Church has not given up its doctrine of plural marriages. It still teaches that doctrine as a Divine revelation, and as imposing a positive duty upon the faithful adherents of the church. It therefore necessarily teaches that the law directed against it is to be resisted or evaded, and that its enforcement is a persecution on account of religious belief. The leaders refuse to distinguish between the practice, which is a crime under the secular laws of all the States and of the Nation, and the doctrine which they hold as an essential article of their creed. This position is of course an entirely consistent one, as the doctrine would be a mere dead letter without the practice. There is no hope of modifying the articles of faith of the

Mormon Church except by rigidly suppressing any practices enjoined by them which are regarded as crimes against social order by civilized communities. Of course it can never be admitted that any sanction of crime can plead religious liberty for a defense. There is only one course open for the Government, and that is, without interfering with the beliefs or the organized systems of the people, to suppress by any legislation that may be found necessary to the purpose and by its rigid enforcement the practice of polygamy in the Territories. By so doing it may secure its formal abandonment, whatever the Mormon authorities may see fit to do with their so-called revelations. They may see a new light in time and conclude that revelations may be repealed by the same authority that establishes them.

The Utah Commission gives its adhesion to the proposition for amending the National Constitution so as to prohibit and punish polygamy throughout the United States. They give as a reason for favoring this that it would advertise to the people of the world the fact that in the United States the practice of polygamy under the cloak of religious belief will not be tolerated in any part of the country. Such an advertisement can hardly be necessary. All the States have laws against this practice which are quite as thoroughly enforced as those against any other form of crime, and Congress has full power to legislate on the subject for the Territories. It can also impose any conditions it may see fit upon the admission of any of the Territories to the Union as States. Rigorous legislation against polygamy in the Territories and its thorough enforcement will be as effective an advertisement to the world as is needed of the policy of the Government on this subject. If the Constitution were to be amended in a way to reach this evil it might as well be done by giving to Congress general jurisdiction on matters of marriage and divorce so as to make the laws relating to these matters uniform for the whole country. Polygamy is at present a local evil, and by a vigorous policy consistently enforced it may be made a temporary one. The Constitution should deal with only the general and permanent interests of the whole people.

The Utah Constitution.

BY THE NEW YORK TIMES | MAY 20, 1895

THE CONSTITUTIONAL CONVENTION of Utah, which assembled in accordance with the enabling act of Congress on the 4th of March, adopted a complete Constitution for the new State on the 6th of May, and it will be submitted to a vote of the people of the Territory for ratification at the general election next November. Some features of this document will excite special interest on account of the peculiar history and at least one "peculiar institution" of the Territory of Utah.

Its most interesting feature, from this point of view, constitutes Article III., and is entitled "Ordinance." It is declared to be "irrevocable without the consent of the United States and the people of this State." Its first paragraph reads: "Perfect toleration of religious sentiment is guaranteed. No inhabitant of this State shall ever be molested in person or property on account of his or her mode of religious worship; but polygamous or plural marriages are forever prohibited." This "ordinance" also includes a declaration that the Legislature shall make laws for the establishment and maintenance of public schools which "shall be open to all the children of the State and be free from sectarian control." This declaration is repeated as the first section of an article of the Constitution relating to education, which also declares that "neither religious nor partisan test or qualification shall be required of any person as a condition of admission as teacher or student in any public educational institution of the State," and that no appropriation of public money shall be made by the State or any civil division or any public corporation "to aid in the support of any school, seminary, academy, college, university, or other institution, controlled in whole or in part by any church, sect, or denomination whatever." Every effort seems to have been made to give assurance in the Constitution that polygamy would not be revived and that no preference or advantage would be allowed to Mormonism in public affairs. There is in the "declaration of rights" the usual guarantee of religious liberty, freedom of conscience, &c., but it contains some unusual phrases, as, for instance, that no church "shall dominate the State or interfere with its functions."

Another interesting feature of this Constitution is the declaration that the rights of citizens to vote and hold office "shall not be denied or abridged on account of sex," and that male and female citizens "shall enjoy equally all civil, political, and religious rights and privileges." It does not say, however, that they shall be subject to the same duties and obligations. No person can vote without having been a citizen of the United States for ninety days before the election.

Among the useful restrictions upon the legislative power is one prohibiting it from passing special laws incorporating cities, towns, or villages or amending their charters. The Legislature must provide by general laws for the "incorporation, organization, and classification of cities and towns in proportion to population," which is a somewhat vague and ambiguous phraseology. There is a limitation put upon the power to incur debt and to impose taxes, by the State and by counties and towns, and a very foolish requirement of a uniform and equal rate of assessment and taxation on all property in the State, property being defined as including "moneys, credits, bonds, stocks, franchises, and all matters and things (real, personal, and mixed) capable of private ownership." Of course, the attempt to apply this will be a failure in Utah, as elsewhere, and will result in the grossest inequality in the collection of taxes.

The Constitution errs, as most recent instruments of the kind do, in trying to do too much, but its faults in that respect are fewer than those of some of the new States.

Religious Persecution to Cease

BY THE NEW YORK TIMES | NOV. 8, 1895

CHATTANOOGA, TENN., NOV. 7. — Five Seventh-Day Adventists on trial at Dayton, Tenn., for Sabbath violation, were yesterday acquitted without the jurors leaving their seats. This is construed to mean a decided revolution in sentiment toward these people by the citizens of Rhea County, where they have a thriving settlement at Graysville.

Notwithstanding that they have heretofore conducted their own defense, refusing to employ a lawyer and have as regularly been found guilty, at this trial Judge Lewis Shepard of Chattanooga and ex-Congressman Snodgrass of Dayton volunteered in their defense, and both made eloquent and successful appeals to the reason as opposed to the prejudices of their mountain neighbors composing the jury. Judge Parks struck at the false base of these prosecutions, which have attracted National attention, in his charge yesterday, in which he broadly intimated that the cases were trumped up on questionable testimony procured at the instigation of witness fee peculators and fee-grabbing officials.

The trials to-day are in all probability the last that will be brought against these people in East Tennessee, for abundance of good lawyers can be secured to defend their cause at any time without fee or request for the sake of religious liberty, which it is declared has been given a vicious blow in Tennessee by the prosecutions.

Against the Salvation Army.

BY THE NEW YORK TIMES | JULY 29, 1899

PHILADELPHIA, JULY 28. — The Superior Court of Pennsylvania to-day handed down an opinion adverse to the Salvation Army, in which the Court maintains that the question of religious freedom is not involved in a case where the public peace is disturbed. The matter came before the court on an appeal of Joseph Garabad from the Luzerne County courts. He is a Salvation Army officer, and was arrested and fined for beating a drum in a manner to disturb the peace. The Court, in its opinion, says:

"Religious liberty does not include the right to introduce and carry out every scheme or purpose which persons see fit to claim as part of their religious system."

It held that the propriety of the practices of a religious association or its judgment as to the use of a drum as part of its services has nothing to do with the case. The streets, the Court said, belonged to the people, and the fact that the defendant's business was lawful did not justify him in annoying the public.

Hearing at Albany for Christian Scientists

SPECIAL TO THE NEW YORK TIMES | JAN. 31, 1901

ALBANY, JAN. 30. — It is within the bounds of temperate statement to say that no more remarkable hearing upon any proposed piece of legislation has ever occurred at the Capitol in Albany than that which was given to-day upon the Bell bill to prevent Christian Scientists from practicing their art. Members of the Legislature oldest in the service here recall nothing so extraordinary. Lawyers who favored the Scientists and their professional lecturer, Carol Norton, besides Dr. Mary Walker, were among the opponents of the bill, while physicians of reputation not only denied the possibility of the cures claimed, but suggested that those who gave credit to them were harboring a hallucination which was a menace to the health and the welfare of the community.

The hearing took place before the Assembly Committee on Public Health, of which Dr. Henry of New York City is the Chairman. It became evident early in the day that no committee room in the Capitol would afford accommodation for a tenth of the number who were interested in the hearing, and therefore it was held in the Assembly Chamber. The hour set for the hearing was 2 o'clock. Long before then the Assembly Chamber was filled by an audience of well-dressed men and women.

The hearing was opened by Assemblyman Bell, who introduced the bill. Mr. Bell said the bill was not of his own construction. It had been framed by the New York County Medical Society and handed to him. Since it had been introduced it had aroused opposition from other persons than the Christian Scientists whose practice of the healing art it was mainly designed to control. The opticians, the patent medicine men, the sellers of artificial limbs, and others had been aroused because of their belief that it would seriously injure if not altogether ruin their business. In order to meet the objections of these people some amendments had been framed by the medical society.

These amendments he offered. Their effect was to satisfy the interests mentioned.

A Mr. Tallman of New York City, who was called a "Judge," was introduced as the first speaker on behalf of the Christian Scientists. He asked the committee if they appreciated the scope of the legislation which they had been called upon to enact. It was an attack, he said, upon the religious liberty of 70,000 men and women of the best culture in New York. The exercise of the healing art in accordance with the teachings of the Bible was a part of the religion of these people. They had built many churches in the State. One recently erected in New York City cost $500,000.

"I myself am not a Christian Scientist," he said, "but I know something of the good of Christian Science, and I am here to testify to it. My wife for years had been afflicted with a disease for which the most skilled physician in the country treated her without affording her any relief. She took up Christian Science, and in a short time she was a well woman. She is here in this hall to-day. My little granddaughter was afflicted with paralysis. The best physicians in New York were consulted. They pronounced her case incurable. She was treated by Christian Science and in a very few days she was restored to perfect health."

A Mr. Lathrop mentioned that doctors of medicine had told him that he was ill, but he was cured by science.

"Didn't you know you were sick?" asked Assemblyman Sanders.

"I had a conscious feeling of being so," was the reply.

Mr. Lathrop said the "Scientists" regarded all conditions as being mental, and do not recognize any contagious diseases or anything of the sort. A spectator who volunteered the information concerning contagious diseases was asked if there was any law or commandment that contagious diseases be reported to the Board of Health.

"No, Sir. There is no such commandment in the Bible that tells us to report a case to the Board of Health," and with applause greeting this remark, the gentleman sat down.

The next speaker for the "scientists" was Henry L. Call. The result of the enactment of the proposed legislation, Mr. Call said, would be to relegate to the criminal classes a large number of the best men and women in the State.

"And for what reason?" he asked. "Because the medical fraternity, which finds its field being invaded, claims that Christian Science is a sham; that Christian Scientists cannot do what they claim to do. But on the contrary, are working harm. Look around at this audience before you. Do they not look like intelligent and respectable people? Nearly every one here has been cured of some disease by the application of Christian Science. I call upon all who have been cured by Christian Science to stand up."

Nearly the whole audience arose. As the "scientists" gazed around upon their hosts they broke into hand-clapping.

W. D. Baldwin, the President of the Otis Elevator Company, said he wished to speak to the committee as a practical man. "No man," Mr. Baldwin said, "was more antagonistic to Christian Science than I was. Yet I stand here to-day to defend it. My wife, who was a confirmed invalid for years, was healed by it. Her cure led me to investigate. My investigation brought belief. For eight years I have taught my children that God is the source of all power; that when they are sick they should go to God for relief. In all that time we have not needed a physician in our house. Are you going to say to me and to others, 'Your children must unlearn what you have taught them; instead of seeking a cure from God, the source of all power, they must seek it from a man.' "

Carol Norton said: "We have no quarrel with the physicians. Many physicians send patients to us to be healed, and some come to us themselves. I think this bill is misnamed. It ought to be entitled, 'A bill to legislate against the omnipotent power of God.' It is an attempt to make null and void the final command of the Saviour before his ascension: 'Go ye unto the world and heal the sick.' "

The opening argument for the medical fraternity was made by Dr. Henry L. Eisner, who was to-day elected President of the State Medical

Society. "All we ask," said Dr. Eisner, "is proficiency on the part of those who seek to treat others for disease. The laws of the State of New York already require that those who seek to practice medicine must pass an examination which is satisfactory to the State Board of Regents before they are given a license. Public health demands that no person should be allowed to practice the healing art who has not the special education which would enable him to properly diagnose disease."

He spoke of the duty of physicians and the advancement they had made in science. They did not believe in one single way of treating diseases, but were after the greatest good for the greatest number. He wanted the same safeguards thrown around the public from scientists as in the practice of medicine. Referring to how the medical fraternity treats contagious diseases he spoke of the cholera burdened ship in New York Harbor in 1892. "Now what would you have done in that case?" he excitedly asked. "Cure it? No, you would have spread it at every door, and flooded the country with it." Regarding the way the "scientists" treated contagious diseases, and protected the public health, he said: "Four or five hours! Why, that is time enough to spread a disease everywhere."

Dr. Eisner read a letter from President Murphy of the Board of Health, in which Mr. Murphy said: "Christian Science as practiced in New York is a great misfortune. I have no doubt that many lives are lost and many will be lost if these people are permitted to practice their doctrine. The claims of these people are simply deplorable."

Dr. Abraham Jacobi addressed the committee briefly. He said he would not be blasphemous enough to believe that any one could claim the light of Jesus and His Apostles in this day. The practices of the Christian Scientists, he said, were a public danger. It was inconceivable to him how men with education and refinement could not see this.

"I am almost ashamed to come here to plead in such a cause," said the doctor: "it is so evidently a matter of common sense that I make you an apology, Mr. Chairman."

Dr. Mary Walker circa 1870. Dr. Walker was awarded the Medal of Honor for her work as a surgeon during the civil war.

Dr. Clark of Buffalo said: "I fail to find anywhere in the Bible that Jesus of Nazareth went up and down the country healing persons at $2 a head."

Prof. Howe of the Buffalo Medical College also spoke, and Attorney Andrews of New York City, counsel for the New York County Medical Society, reviewed the legal status of Christian Science, touching on cases where convictions had been had for deaths occurring from practicing it.

Dr. Mary Walker spoke in defense of Christian Science. She said: "The legislation proposed against these people is all wrong. They are good people. They come up to my standard of morality and nobody has ever questioned that. If they can heal without the use of medicine, let them do it. I haven't got enough of Jesus in me to do that; but some of these people seem to have. Then why not let them."

The hearing will be resumed again next week.

'Healer' to Be Prosecuted

BY THE NEW YORK TIMES | JAN. 31, 1901

THE BOARD OF HEALTH has at last determined to prosecute Charles G. Pease, the Christian Science "healer," for breaking the law in failing to report cases of contagious disease which have come under his so-called treatment. Pease has for a long time styled himself a doctor. It is charged by the Board of Health that the man has at various times practiced medicine without being registered, and he will also be prosecuted on this charge.

President Murphy of the Health Board has instructed Officer Gillespie to serve a summons on Pease, commanding him to appear before the Magistrate at the West Side Police Court at 2 o'clock this afternoon and show cause why he should not be punished for violating Section 153 of the Sanitary Code in failing to report a case of contagious disease.

The summons, according to President Murphy, is based on the testimony elicited during the recent contest in the Surrogates' Court over the will of Miss Helen C. Brush, who left the bulk of her estate to the First Church of Christ, Scientist. The brother of the testatrix alleged that the "healers" of this church had brought to bear undue influence upon his sister to induce her to make the will. Pease, in his testimony given at the hearings of this case, said that he had abandoned the practice of medicine, and that he did sometimes act as a "healer."

When asked if he reported contagious diseases to the Board of Health, he said that he did not, but he admitted having attended several cases. He further admitted that he had signed death certificates without having attended the patients, which is in direct violation of the law. He said he had visited Miss Brush, but not as a physician, yet he signed the certificate setting forth that she had died of consumption.

President Murphy has secured a transcript of the testimony given by Pease in this case, and it will be used against him at the hearing to-day. In speaking of the case yesterday, Mr. Murphy said:

"The department has been after Pease for two years, and we think now we have enough evidence to convict him."

Religious Liberty in Alaskan Islands

BY MAX J. KOHLER | SEPT. 10, 1905

CONGRESS WAS RECENTLY engaged in framing and enacting a special code of laws for Alaska. The peculiar conditions there existing have been recognized from the start by our Government, and in consequence Alaska has remained longer than any other of our dominions in a state of tutelage as an unorganized Territory. Special treatment of that Territory was requisite, not merely because the land, unlike our other previously acquired domains, was detached from the rest of our territory, but because the anomalous character of these new inhabitants, obviously required novel, special treatment. In these respects our experiences with Alaska and our legislation respecting her may become significant precedents for our treatment of our newly acquired cessions from Spain.

Questions that have complicated our treatment of Alaskans with respect to religious liberty are also likely to arise with respect to our new possessions. In view of these circumstances, the curious incident herein to be considered may be of special interest to-day.

An examination of some Treasury Department correspondence made a few years ago in connection with some pending Government litigation brought to light the various unpublished Government reports and documents herein considered, bearing upon this curious chapter in the history of the relations of Church and State in America.

It will be remembered that the Pribilof Islands, known also as the Alaskan Seal Islands, a group consisting of the two small islands named St. Paul and St. George, lying west of the Alaskan mainland, became United States territory as part of the Alaskan cession of 1867 from Russia, and that these islands have been of importance far beyond what their size and products would seem to warrant, because they are annually visited by herds of fur seals that establish their rookeries there. This fact became the basis for Mr. James C. Carter's interesting argument before the International Fur Seal Arbitration Tribunal of 1893, that the seals are domestic animals, established on land here and returning annually to their "fixed homes" here after periodical, temporary, aquatic migrations, and that, therefore, the very valuable Alaskan sealskin industry is an American domestic institution belonging to the United States.

At the time of the Alaskan cession there were approximately three hundred native residents on the Pribilof Islands, about the same number as are now living there, about two-thirds of whom dwell on the larger of the two islands, St. Paul. These natives are Aleutians by descent, but intermarriage with Russian and American stock during several generations has materially modified the appearance and racial characteristics of these people. At the time of the cession to the United States they were devout believers in the faith of the Greco-Roman Church, and their piety and steadfastness to this creed have not abated during the American occupancy, as will more clearly appear hereinafter. Our treaty with Russia, embodying the cession, contained several provisions designed to protect and secure these natives in the exercise of their religious observances. Thus, in Article II. it was provided:

> It is, however, understood and agreed that the churches which have been built in the ceded territory by the Russian Government shall remain the property of such members of the Greek Oriental Church resident in the territory as may choose to worship therein.

And Article III. provides that the inhabitants of the ceded territory "with the exception of uncivilized native tribes, shall be admitted to the enjoyment of all the rights, advantages, and immunities of citizens of the United States, and shall be maintained and protected in the free enjoyment of their liberty, property, and religion. The uncivilized tribes will be subject to such laws and regulations as the United States may from time to time adopt in regard to aboriginal tribes of that country."

In view of these express provisions, it is unnecessary to inquire for our present purposes whether the first amendment of the Federal Constitution prohibiting Congress from making any law respecting an establishment of religion or prohibiting the free exercise thereof, applies of its own force to these islands, though it is not without interest to observe that Secretary of the Treasury Charles Foster, in 1891, in his "instructions" to the Treasury Agent placed in charge of the islands, wrote: "You will endeavor to secure the good-will and confidence of the native inhabitants of the islands and advise them whenever practicable of their rights and duties as American citizens, and by proper means try to increase their friendship for the Government and the people of the United States."

The Pribilof Islands were discovered about 1787, and their value in connection with the fur seal industry was soon realized by the Russians. Many thousands of fur seals had been taken annually on these islands by the Russians prior to the cession, and that Government had farmed out the islands to a company engaged in this industry, and thus granted exclusive rights over the islands some time before 1867. Our Government continued this system, and treated the right to take fur seals on the Pribilof Islands as a Government monopoly, to be granted to private parties in consideration of rentals to be paid to the United States, and turned the islands into a Government reservation, upon which it was unlawful for any persons other than the resident natives to enter without express Government authority.

During the period from 1870 to 1890 the Government's lessee, the Alaska Commercial Company, took and shipped about 100,000 fur seal skins per annum from the islands, and the natives were paid pursuant to the contract made by this company with the Government, 40 cents per skin, for their labor in driving, killing, skinning, and curing these animals. The consequence was that these few hundred natives had, relatively speaking, large means at their disposal, which enabled them to purchase numerous articles of luxury at the company's stores on the island. For nearly all their luxuries and necessities of life the islanders are wholly dependent upon the United States, for their soil is barren and unproductive, and the Governmental policy of maintaining this group as a Government reservation isolates the natives from all other people, prevents them from trading and trafficking with other persons, and places their labor solely at the disposal of the Government and its lessees, except in so far as, within very limited spheres, it is possible for them to make personal efforts for the improvement of their own condition through their own manual labor.

The Government has recognized its obligations to the islanders, and made provisions for their welfare in the subsisting twenty-year lease with the North American Commercial Company, entered into in 1890, which is even more advantageous in theory for them than was the former lease to the Alaska Commercial Company. By this lease the Government receives an annual rental, subject to certain abatements, of $60,000, and in addition $9.62 ½ for every skin shipped from the island by the lessees. The lessees provide the natives under this lease with dried salmon and salt for preserving meat, also eighty tons of coal annually, sufficient numbers of comfortable dwelling houses to be occupied by the natives, a suitable schoolhouse and instruction for the children of the inhabitants, as well as a suitable house for religious worship; also competent physicians and medicine and necessaries of life for the widows and orphans and aged and infirm inhabitants. Compensation at the rate of 50 cents per skin is paid by the company to the natives for their work in taking, killing, and curing the seals. This payment is commonly made in the form of credit on the books of the lessee company, against which credits the natives are charged with the articles they purchase at the company's stores. Of course the cost of transporting articles such a distance is very great.

The very great reduction in the size of the herd of fur seals resulting from pelagic sealing and the necessary reduction of the company's quota on this account limited by the Government, have very greatly reduced the earnings of the natives, since only a small fraction of the one-time annual quota of 100,000 seals can now be taken. In fact, during the seasons of 1891, 1892, and 1893, pending the convocation and awards of the Fur Seal International Tribunal at Paris, the American quota was limited by a treaty with England to 7,500 seals per annum. The consequence was that new measures were necessary for the support and maintenance of the natives, and accordingly Congress has been appropriating $19,500 per annum for this purpose, which sum is disbursed by the Treasury Department for the benefit of the natives. The result is that during the past fourteen years these natives have been, as never before, public charges, dependent upon the Government, if not for actual sustenance, at least for all the comforts and conveniences of civilization, and many would no doubt be unable to sustain life even were it not for this Governmental assistance.

Mr. Joseph Stanley-Brown, who was for several years Treasury Agent on these islands, and subsequently became Superintendent of the present lessees, has well described certain characteristics of these natives, which must be understood before the bearings of the problem in mind can be profitably considered. He describes them thus:

A generous infusion of Caucasian blood has done much to obliterate the line of descent, but it is evident at a glance that their progenitors were people of short, thick bodies, little-used legs, high cheekbones, horizontal, not slanting eyes, coarse black hair, and skin tanned by sun and wind. ... Although these natives affect the garments of civilization, there still lingers an occasional article of wearing apparel that links them to aboriginal days. ... They are docility personified, and with them, 'Whatever is, is right.' Violent language or physical force is unknown save when under the influence of liquor. As they are human beings, they have the failings to which all flesh is heir. They are susceptible to flattery, very vulnerable to ridicule, fond of finery, fail in a just appreciation of the value of money, have not solved the problem of thrift, and do not know how to make both ends meet. The one characteristic that stands out prominently above all others is their devotion to the Greek Church. It is extraordinary that the Russians should have been able to implant in the hearts of these people, by bribery and compulsion, such an absolute, all-enveloping devotion to their faith. The ceremonial of the Greek Church is peculiarly fitted to captivate the aboriginal mind, and its hold upon the imagination and the loyalty of the Aleuts is complete. It is certainly unfortunate that an orga-nization which holds them in such complete subjection, and which is the solace and comfort of their monotonous lives, is not exercised for their improvement in the direction of the ordinary moralities of life.

Reference has already been made to the fact that in the contract made by the lessees with the United States, the former expressly obli-gated themselves to maintain the Church on the islands. It would no doubt astonish many citizens of the United States to learn that the Government has entered into a contract looking to the maintenance of a church of the Greek Catholic faith within its dominions, as one of the considerations of a contract moving to the Government. One can read-ily understand the desirability of inducing these Government "wards" to continue under religious tenets, tending to lift them above sav-agery and improving their moral condition, but it may well be doubted whether such contract is not contrary to our constitutional provisions relative to religious liberty. (See *Bradfield vs. Roberts.* 26 Washington Law Reporter, Page 84, reported on appeal 175, U. S., 291.)

More serious friction in practice was caused by the circumstance that the ritual and observances of the Greek Church tend to check the "Americanization" of the natives and their adoption of English as their vernacular, and that the marriage laws of that Church with respect to prohibited consanguineous marriages, lead to absurd or disastrous results among such a very small community, the members of which are so closely related to each other, and to which migration of other persons is prohibited. Thus, already in 1889, Special Agent Loud, who was in charge of St. George, the smaller of the two islands, in his report to the Secretary of the Treasury said:

I have no hesitancy in saying that the rules and regulations of the Greek Church are detrimental to the welfare of the people toward civilization. The natives built and occupy the church and they pay the priest and support his family, and yet they are compelled to send annually large sums to the Greek Church at San Francisco, which, under the circum-stances, is little less than robbery. The rule which compels people to leave

a warm house in the early morning of a cold Winter's day to stand in a
church that had never a fire nor any means to make it, should be altered,
if possible, for it is the cause of more colds, coughs, and sickness here
than all other things combined. The marriage law of the Church becomes
an absurdity when enforced on this island, and is the direct cause of
much misery to young and old alike. The most distant relationship is
sufficient cause to prevent a marriage, and consequently this must lead
to bad results on an island where the population is less than 100. My own
observations prove to me that this is the cause of a great deal of wrong
and immorality.

In 1889 the condition of the seal herds was so serious that the Treasury Agent in charge recommended that the taking of seals on the island should be wholly prohibited for several years. The total extermination of the seals seemed imminent, and with them the means of livelihood of the natives. The new lease for 1890 provided that only 60,000 seals should be taken that year, but in fact the Government agent permitted the capture of only about 20,000, as more could not be taken without danger to the herd. In 1891, by a convention with England, the United States agreed to permit only 7,500 seals to be taken that year. The future of the natives, as well as of the seals, was precarious, and Government appropriations for the benefit of the natives could not be counted upon. Ordinary prudence required that the natives should economize and husband their resources, and liberality with the property that was ostensibly their own, was in fact simply increasing the amount of the Government's prospective disbursements on their behalf. When Government appropriations were made eventually the money was distributed so as to assist the natives, only after they had exhausted their own means and in the endeavor to maintain in them a sense of independence and of self-support. It was this period that was selected by an official of the Greek Church to procure collections and contributions for religious purposes from these shiftless public charges, the money to be used outside of the islands. Nearly $1,300 had been contributed for this purpose by the natives of St. George, and about $3,325 had been subscribed by the inhabitants of St. Paul when the Government Agent learned of these facts and directed the lessees to withhold the latter sum from the ecclesiastic who had secured the same, Bishop Vladimir, pending instructions from the department. In his official report to the Treasury Department, dated Dec. 3, 1891, Treasury Agent William H. Williams wrote relative to this matter:

> As the natives are without sufficient means of support for the ensuing year, and the Government will be called upon to assist them, I regard the taking of this money from them as an outrage, which should not be permitted. I am informed that it has been the practice for the islands to be visited at stated periods by persons claiming to have some religious authority, who demand from the natives a part of their earnings. Not a dollar is ever returned to them, but it is taken out of the country and said to be used in private speculation. I understand that an effort was made to have this so-called Bishop, above referred to, consent to a part of the money being used in the education and maintenance of some orphans who are now being supported by charity at the Ounalaska School, but the greed and avarice of this man would be satisfied with nothing but Shylock measures. He should never have been permitted to come upon the islands, and the lessees and the revenue cutters should be made to understand that they must land no one on the islands without the consent of the Secretary of the Treasury or the Government Agent in charge.

The following year the Secretary of the Treasury, in his instructions to the Treasury Agent in charge, under date of May 2, 1892, accordingly wrote:

> [...] for the Church failed utterly in all matters of courtesy when calling at the island last Summer. His coming was welcomed by the Government officials, they believing that it would furnish them an opportunity for conference, looking to the welfare of the natives, but he made no effort to acquaint himself from reliable sources with the condition of the natives, nor manifested the slightest concern as to their progress or material welfare while he did not even call at the village of St. George, from which no contributions could be expected.
>
> That the natives do not feel especially aggrieved by the return of the money is indicated by the fact that they, to an individual, accepted it, realizing, as they did, their needy condition.

Government's Action no Interference with Religious Liberty — This
action of the Government cannot justly be construed as interference with
the religious liberty of the people, but must be looked at in the light of an
attempt merely to protect its wards.

The redistribution of this money among the natives did not end this matter, however. The Greek Church authorities lost little time in making demands on the North American Commercial Company for the payment of this money, and, as the company had received the money from the Bishop, to whom it belonged in law, simply for the purpose of having it transmitted to San Francisco, and its delivery to the Government was not authorized by the Church authorities, counsel for the company advised that it could not legally resist the claim of the consistory of the Greek Church at San Francisco for its payment.

Soon afterward the Russian Minister at Washington made demands upon the United States through the State Department relative to this matter, and the specific claim was made that this was a violation of the religious liberty clauses of the treaty of cession above referred to. The upshot of the matter was that Secretary of the Treasury Carlisle, on March 24, 1894, recommended to Congress that an appropriation be made for the payment of this money, and he officially stated that he was "of opinion that the contention of the Russian Minister is a proper one."

Congress thereupon in that same year provided that $3,325 of the $19,500 appropriated for the support of the natives that year "shall be paid to the Bishop of the Greek Church, San Francisco, Calif., in full satisfaction of that amount contributed by members of said Church of said island, and placed in the hands of the agent of the north American Commercial Company for delivery to the Bishop of said Church, and afterward under instructions of the Treasury Department expended in furnishing the natives of said island necessary supplies to prevent suffering and starvation, a pro rata amount being allowed each of the families on said island," (28 Statutes at Large, Page 391).

The annual appropriations of the Government for the support of these natives continue, but nothing prevents these public charges from continuing their generosity toward their Church officials at the public expense, and thus indirectly using public moneys for sectarian religious purposes. The recommendations of the Treasury Agents were ignored, and the measures adopted at their instance to prevent a recurrence of these incidents were superseded, when, in 1895, the Secretary of the Treasury, in his "instructions" to the agent in charge, after advising him of the Congressional appropriation for the reimbursement of the Greek Church, added:

> *The order heretofore made by the department prohibiting the collection of money from the natives for transmission to places outside of the Territory has been revoked. But it will be your duty to see that no coercive means are employed by any person to secure contributions of money from the natives, and to advise them that they are at liberty to make such contributions as they choose, but the same must be in all cases entirely voluntary on their part.*

It will have been observed that the principle of religious liberty was invoked on behalf of the Greek Church authorities to prevent Governmental interference with their securing contributions from the natives, but it may well be doubted whether our American doctrine of separation of Church and State is not in fact being violated by the continuance of such collections with the Government's passive consent.

Quakers Pledge Aid to Nation in War

BY THE NEW YORK TIMES | MAY 29, 1917

PREFERRING WHAT THEY called the martyrdom of refusing military duty to exemption from war service, many Quakers who were present at the joint meeting of the orthodox and liberal factions of the Religious Society of Friends at the Friends Meeting House, at 144 East Twentieth Street last night, hesitated to support a resolution recording their appreciation of the Government's action in excluding them from the draft. The resolution was finally adopted, but not until certain of the Quaker leaders, including President Isaac Sharpnell of Haverford College, had declared that they did not believe that exemption from the draft was very much desired, because it deprived the Quakers of their much cherished privilege of suffering for their convictions. The Quakers agreed to assist the Government by work of a constructive nature during the war and to take steps to prevent "slackers" from joining the order to escape military service.

The Quakers agreed also not to admit applicants for membership of military age.

"The best advertisement that our movement could have," said President Sharpnell, "is the possibility of being able to stand up for liberty of conscience. Personally, I do not think that exemption will be a good thing. On the contrary I think it would be a good thing if all our young Quakers should go to jail. In this way, by making the Government feel that we are ready to suffer and die for our convictions, we perpetuate our ideals and pass them on to future generations."

During the discussion of this very point prior to the adoption of the resolution, Carolina Woods said that the nearest avenue to martyrdom left to the Quakers now was to lend all their support and sympathy to conscientious objectors who were not identified with any religious body and whose individual objections would not be recognized by the Government as grounds for exemption.

"We ought not feel proud of our exemption," said Miss Woods. "By exempting us the Government has merely deprived us of the privilege of suffering for our convictions, the privilege of suffering for our ideals which we prize so dearly. The opportunity for suffering can only come to us now by standing with other conscientious objectors who are not exempt, by standing beside them in tribunals and lending our voice to theirs and by visiting them in prisons."

MEETING A HISTORIC ONE.

Last night's meeting was historic in Quaker annals because it was the first time since 1828 that the liberal and orthodox wings of the Religious Society of Friends have come together in a joint meeting. In 1828 the Quakers of this country split on the question of the divinity of Christ, the orthodox members of the Church holding firmly to the doctrine of the Trinity and the liberals making a pronounced departure toward unitarianism.

Yesterday, however, on the ground that Quakers could preach a message of peace and love to the world only by first being at peace among themselves, the orthodox Quakers assembled in their yearly meeting at 144 East Twentieth Street, invited their liberal brethren who were holding a separate yearly meeting in the Friends' Meeting House at Rutherford Place and East Fifteenth Street to forget their differences for the time being and join them in a united effort to bring good-will and love into the hearts of men.

According to some of the leading Quakers present, the reunion of last night was merely a forerunner of a complete reconciliation of the two factions of Friends throughout the country, especially inasmuch as the theological questions involved in their ancient dispute had been retired more or less to the background as dead issues.

The joint meeting was presided over by Elwood Burdsall of the liberal group and James Wood of the orthodox faction. From the moment the meeting opened the discussion centred on the exemption of the Quakers from military service. Owing to the unusually large number of applicants who have sought admission to the Society of Friends within the last three days, several Quakers gave utterance to the suspicion that some of them might be "slackers" who were trying to avoid military service.

CAUTIOUS ABOUT NEW MEMBERS.

Earlier in the day, at the meeting of the Liberal Friends, former Congressman W. W. Cocks of Westbury, L. I., expressed himself on this point in the following manner:

> This is a poor time to take in members of military age. If we want to maintain our reputation in our stand on peace, let us render such service to our Government as our consciences will permit. There are many ways to offer valuable service, just as valuable as the work of the men in the trenches. We are in war and must now play the part of the good Samaritan, but we must see to it that the Jericho road is rid of thieves.

Within the last three days there have been eighteen applications for admission to the liberal branch of the Society of Friends in this city, and more than thirty applications for admission to the orthodox group. In normal times a Yearly Meeting of either body would bring no more than half a dozen new members.

It was said yesterday that all new applications would receive very careful consideration, and that no man would be received into the society on the basis of mere opposition to war or military service alone. Before becoming eligible the applicant will have to show a thorough understanding and appreciation of all the other principles and ideals to which the Friends are devoted. As for the mass of recent applications, it was stated at the joint meeting last night that most of them were from persons, women and men, who were above military age.

In formulating their resolution, the Quakers considered very seriously the advisability of incorporating a clause that would assure the Government that the Society of Friends would bar all men of draft age from its ranks until after the war, but when it was made clear that the exemption applied only to men who were members of the society when the law was passed the Friends opposed the clause as unnecessary and possibly offensive to young men within the draft age who were conscientiously converted to Quaker ideals.

RESOLUTION THANKS CONGRESS.

As finally adopted the resolution read as follows:

> The New York Yearly Meetings of the Religious Society of Friends place upon record their appreciation of the recognition of religious convictions by the national Congress in exempting from military service the members of our society, and our further recognition that this action places upon us a serious responsibility to see that no improper use is made of this exemption.
>
> We realize that the recent discussion of the Christian ideals of war and peace has drawn toward us many earnest souls who may through this approach come to a full understanding of our principles and bring to us fresh strength and courage. We therefore recommend that monthly meetings exercise unusual care and sympathetic encouragement in such cases.
>
> We are united in expressing our love for our country and our desire to serve her loyally. We offer our service to the Government of the United States in any constructive work in which we can conscientiously serve.

Efforts were made by some Quakers to have the resolutions include a formal expression of regret that the Government did not extend the privilege of exemption to other conscientious objectors as well as the Quakers. But ex-Congressman Cocks vigorously opposed the amendment on the ground that it was "looking a gift horse in the mouth."

Although conscientiously opposed to taking up arms, the Quakers agreed last night that they would have ample opportunity to serve the country by doing a lot of constructive work. This means that they will be active in relief and ambulance work and also in farming. They will co-operate with Friends in England and France to ascertain how they can also be of service in those countries.

Conscientious Objectors

BY THE NEW YORK TIMES | FEB. 16, 1919

FROM THE WAY one great event crowds another off the stage at Washington in swift succession it would be thought that such a comparatively minor affair as the discharge of 113 conscientious objectors would soon pass into oblivion. A few days after the announcement that the Secretary of War had ordered these 113 men released from the disciplinary barracks at Fort Leavenworth, with an honorable discharge from the army, with full pay, all the stir of interest aroused at first began to die away. But later the episode exhibited an unsuspected power of revival. It is now being discussed in a way that indicates a Congressional investigation of the whole handling of the conscientious objector problem by the War Department.

Within the last few days a resolution has been introduced in the House calling on Secretary Baker to send to that body a statement of the number of conscientious objectors discharged and the reasons for their dismissal. From many parts of the country protests have come to Washington. These, mostly in the form of letters from individuals, have a ring of sincere indignation over the contrast between these men who refused to fight going forth free with from $300 to $500 back pay in their pockets and soldiers who fought returning home crippled with but a few dollars in their pockets.

There are members of Congress who assert that friendly influence was at work in the War Department to shield the conscientious objector beyond what was his due; that in order to accomplish this those in control went far in a policy of increasing leniency toward the objectors; that the conscientious objectors became aware of this and, therefore, more and more defiant of military authority; that it was this exasperating attitude on the part of the conscientious objectors which finally brought upon some of them the rough treatment they received.

STATEMENT BY AN OFFICER.

One of the members of Congress who makes these assertions is Representative T. A. Chandler of Oklahoma. He has been carrying on an inquiry into the affair at Fort Leavenworth and has come into possession of "A Statement of Facts Pertaining to the Conditions Which Arose Between the Military Authorities and the Conscientious Objectors, by Eugene C. Brisbin, Captain of Infantry, U. S. A., Office of Provost Marshal, Camp Funston, Kan., Jan. 8, 1919." Mr. Chandler declines to make known how he got hold of the report for fear of involving innocent persons, but says that it was evidently made in pursuance of instructions from a superior officer, and that it reveals the inside of the handling of the conscientious objectors problem by the War Department.

"There is only one explanation for the course that has been followed from the first with these objectors," said Mr. Chandler in Washington the other day.

Some one at the War Department was in close sympathy with these men. In securing for them lenient treatment various orders were issued by the War Department that were in clear conflict with the law. What these orders were, how previous instructions were amended by confidential letters, are set forth in Captain Brisbin's report.

To begin at the beginning: The law as amended by Congress May 18, 1917, for the express purpose of closing the door on slackers, exempted from combatant service but one limited class — members of well recognized religious sects existing at that time, (note the word 'existing,') to close the door on slackers, pacifists, and so forth who might try to get up some new organization. The sects exempted were those whose beliefs forbid them to participate in war. The law adds, 'but no person so exempted shall be exempted from service in any capacity that the President shall declare noncombative.'

The law contains nothing that could be construed to mean that drafted men would be permitted to walk around camp in civilian clothing, yet the report of Captain Brisbin shows that the first instructions under the law to the army from the War Department exempted a certain class of men from wearing uniforms. Here are the exact words of the order, dated Sept. 25, 1917:

'The Secretary of War directs that selected Mennonites who report to your camp for duty be not forced to wear uniform, as question of raiment is one of the tenets of their faith.'

On Oct. 10 came another change. This is from a letter from the War Department to division commanders, sent out with the injunction that under no circumstances were the instructions contained therein to be given to the newspapers:

'With reference to their attitude to objecting to military service these men (conscientious objectors) are not to be treated as violating military laws, thereby subjecting them to penalties of the Articles of War, but their attitude in this respect will be quietly ignored, and they will be treated with kindly consideration. Attention to this connection is invited to a case where a number of conscientious objectors in one of our divisions, when treated in this manner, renounced their original objections to military service and voluntarily offered to give their best efforts to the United States as soldiers.'

"Now," said Mr. Chandler,

if these men were to be treated as not violating military law when they did, what control was there to be over them? What can you hope to do with men when you 'quietly ignore' their refusal to meet the demands of the simplest necessary discipline?

What came next? This — although the statute clearly defines the term 'conscientious objector,' we find a confidential letter from the Secretary of War, dated Dec. 19, 1917, extending this meaning beyond what Congress intended. By this letter, sent to all camp commanders except the commander of Camp Grant, any drafted man who had 'personal scruples' against war was to be classed as a conscientious objector. Any one can see how wide this opened the door to slacking. The letter, taken from Captain Brisbin's statement, is worth reading word for word. It is as follows:

'1. The Secretary of War directs that, until further instructions on the subject are issued, "personal scruples against war" should be construed as constituting "conscientious objectors," and such persons should be treated in the same manner as other 'conscientious objectors' under the institutions contained in confidential letter from this office dated Oct. 10, 1917.

'2. Under no circumstances should these instructions be communicated to the newspapers.'

"Later came an order interfering with the assignment of the conscientious objectors to noncombatant service," and Mr. Chandler read from the statement an order sent out in a War Department letter April 18, 1918. It contained the following:

> The Secretary of War directs the attention of all commanding officers to the provisions of Paragraph 3 of this order to the effect that no punitive hardship of any kind be imposed on conscientious objectors who do not accept assignment to noncombatant service before the cases shall have been submitted to the Secretary of War and instructions relating to their disposition shall have been issued by him.

This memorandum from the Secretary of War to the Adjutant General was published the same day:

> Mr. Keppel (Third Assistant Secretary of War) has brought to my attention the question raised in my absence as to whether men who accept service in noncombatant branches under the provisions of the President's Executive order shall be required to bear side arms.

'FAR BEYOND INTENTION OF LAWMAKERS.'

> 'My judgment is that it should be contrary to the spirit of the order to require these men to bear arms if they cannot conscientiously do so.'
> Captain Brisbin says in his statement that the side arms referred to in this memorandum," explained Mr. Chandler, "consisted of a belt, with bayonet and scabbard, worn as a rule to designate men on certain duties.

In summarizing the law and regulations relating to conscientious objectors, Captain Brisbin states, after reviewing the additional instructions given to the Secretary's Board of Inquiry for constitutional objectors:

> A careful study of the above instructions and orders issued concerning the conscientious objector, in comparison with the law under which such instructions have been issued, clearly shows that those controlling the issuance of such instructions went far beyond the intention of the lawmakers in many instances. ... Add to the few religious objectors

contemplated in the law the pacifists, cowards, disloyalists and others who desire to avoid military service or to interfere in every way with the proper disciplining of the army, and the result is that, in each of the training camps, there are to be found several hundred of these men doing nothing to assist in the prosecution of the war. The presence of these men in camp, privileged as indicated in the above instructions, injuriously affects the discipline of the entire command.

It was never intended by the Legislature that any citizen of the United States should be exempted from service during the existing emergency. It was not their intention that any class of soldiers should be drafted into the United States Army and encouraged to claim exemption from military service by simply stating their conscientious objections.

"Two cases in Captain Brisbin's 'Statement of Facts,' which follows his 'Statement of the Law,' are worthy of note," said Mr. Chandler in running his eye over the part referred to.

One of the first five conscientious objectors that showed up at Camp Funston announced that he was a conscientious objector and that he did not care who knew it, that he had reached this decision of his own free will after having held consultation with God. Upon investigation it was found that this man had served two or three years in the Missouri National Guard, part of the time on the Mexican border.

Another case is that of Lester G. Ott, for striking whom, when he refused to assist in cleaning up, Sergeant John Bell of the Military Police Company at Fort Leavenworth is to be brought to trial under the Ninth Article of War. Ott, according to the statement of Major John L. Stettinius, Judge Advocate, early in 1918 became a member of the Cincinnati Home Guard and served with it as an armed sentinel and, as a member of the guard, he took an oath to support and defend the Constitution against all the enemies of the United States. Later, when drafted, Ott turned up as a conscientious objector.

INCREASE OF OBJECTORS.

Naturally under a policy of increasing leniency the number of 'conscientious objectors' at the camps increased, Captain Brisbin says, in the report: 'It was literature and handbills of this kind (some of it from *religious organizations on conscientious objections, other plain German propaganda aimed at disaffection in the army) distributed around the camps and through many of the organizations which soon caused a marked increase in the number of so-called conscientious objectors; so, from Jan. 1, 1918, the number increased from a mere handful until up to a few days ago there were 553 in this camp, and it is very surprising to know that of those 553 only 21 have been so disobedient or so antagonistic to any military authority whatever that it has forced the proper authorities to take action against them. This action has been made necessary by two important factors, for both of which the responsibility may be placed on the men themselves.*

(a) Their complete and whole-hearted belief in these handbills or German propaganda which were spread through the camps.

(b) They all rest assured, in their own mind, that nothing can happen to them, as they have a great friend in Washington, Mr. Keppel, the Third Assistant Secretary of War, who will support them, 'so they state,' in anything their conscience tells them to do; and all other military authorities are to be considered their enemies; therefore, the hardships brought to bear on the guards over them, and their superior officers, due to this extreme narrow-mindedness, or in some cases, I might say, state of cowardice, have been of such a nature, at the same time taking into consideration the War Department's instructions, that an officer or enlisted man having any connection with them whatsoever is called upon to do the impossible, and I do not believe these men were treated with any more disrespect in other camps than they were in this one; but, nevertheless, upon using the utmost precaution and tact in the handling of these men, opposition was received at every turn of the wheel from one source or another.

REPORT OF LIEUT. COL. WILLIAMS.

As further testimony on the effect of such lenient treatment on those who called themselves 'conscientious objectors,' I quote from a report, included in Captain Brisbin's statement, made by Lieut. Col. S. M. Williams, Camp Inspector on the General Staff at Camp Funston, under date of Oct. 14, 1918:

'Pursuant to verbal instructions from headquarters, Camp Funston, I this day made an investigation of the treatment received by alleged

conscientious objectors now in the guardhouse at this camp. From my visit to the guardhouse I found in one cell of ample space eighteen of these men. One was found to be confined in a room by himself in another part of the guardhouse. It appears, in fact, that these men are mutineers, although under the law they probably couldn't be tried for mutiny. They absolutely and positively refuse to obey any military order or any instruction that appears in any way to be from a military source. They are determined to follow their own inclination and show an utter disregard and contempt for any military rule or regulation imposed upon them. This condition makes it extremely hard for the guard over them properly to handle them.

'If they are told to take a bath, they will or they won't as they see fit. They will not march to meals in any orderly formation. If they are to go in or out of a door and decide in so doing they are obeying a military order, they refuse to do so. Any number of other instances may be quoted to show their attitude toward the military authorities and the Government. Their attitude is extremely exasperating to those who are required to guard and care for them. This has caused, possibly, in some instances an overamount of force used to require them to perform necessary things. It is very difficult, particularly for enlisted men over them, to handle these men with gentleness, kindness, and firmness to the proper degree.

'I have no desire to excuse officers, noncommissioned officers, and privates who overstepped the line in the treatment of these conscientious objectors, and for which they are to stand trial by court-martial, but I ask to what were they to resort to make these men do the necessary things required of men in confinement? By a series of orders and instructions from Washington the objectors had been exempted from the regulations by which the other prisoners were controlled. All the way through a preference had been shown to these people. Whatever the source of this favoring influence, the result was to make it harder and harder for the officers in charge of the objectors.

'I contend that if a set of just rules had been laid down by the War Department at the start, and the officers in charge had been permitted to follow these without interference, there would never have been any mistreatment. The conditions that were laid down from Washington, a policy always veering toward the constitutional objector, made inevitable a state of increasing exasperation. If the War Department had stuck to the law passed by Congress there would have been even less likelihood of mistreatment, and the door to slacking would have been closed.'

CALLS RELEASE AN "OUTRAGE."

"I think the release of these 113 conscientious objectors was an outrage," exclaimed Mr. Chandler.

I cannot use any gentler term than that. Why should these men who refused to do a soldier's duty be discharged, in full standing and with full pay, while there remained at the same prison 3,500 men, some of whom had seen service on the battleline in France and many of them there for some trivial offense?

At the same time we witness thousands of the boys in the army, both in the camps here and in foreign countries, who have stood ready and willing to fight for their country, trying to obtain discharge to return to needed duties in civil life and being denied, while these so-called conscientious objectors are given preference. The men who stood ready to make the supreme sacrifice on the battlefield must step aside while objectors, with from $300 to $600 back pay, pass honorably out of the army. What will the thousands of men in uniform think of Mr. Baker and his assistants as these facts come to them?

And it is being brought home in many parts of this country every day now. I have a case before me — that of an expert driller. You know we have the oil industry down in my part of the country, and this man, who is now in the army and who has done his full duty while there, has thus far been unable to get out. Especially is this felt when preference is given to such a conscientious objector as Henry Layman. I have a transcript of some of his testimony when he was examined at Camp Funston. He said he was born in Russia.

'Do you read your Bible in Russian or in American?' he was asked.

'No, in German,' was the answer.

Should this man be given a preference over our good American boys who fought in France? Any one who reads the list of names of those discharged from Fort Leavenworth will observe what a large percentage of German names it contained. At the least, these men should have been kept until peace was declared. I think this whole affair should be probed to the bottom to find out the real source of this unfair protection, to see whether German propagandists and sympathizers were taking advantage of this situation to foment dissatisfaction and disturbance over the conscientious objectors problem.

The people — the plain people back home — are stirred up much more over this than we in Washington fully realize.

Mr. Chandler asked his secretary for a letter from the file. "This," he said, "is the kind of letters Congressmen are receiving. You will see that it is a spontaneous outburst from a man not accustomed to letter writing to public officials. The writer is a farmer in Oklahoma. He says:

> 'Now, for one, I am strongly opposed to the action of Mr. Baker taking those undue advantages of the American soldier. It is, in my opinion, a direct insult to the uniform of this nation. ... Now I for one denounce the action of Mr. Baker and believe the people of the country are with me in the thought.'

Representative Norman J. Gould of New York introduced the resolution that the Secretary of War send to Congress a statement of the number of conscientious objectors discharged and the reasons for their dismissal.

High Court Voids Jehovah Sect Curb

SPECIAL TO THE NEW YORK TIMES | MAY 21, 1940

WASHINGTON, MAY 20 — In a unanimous opinion, delivered by Justice Roberts, the Supreme Court today reversed the conviction of three members of Jehovah's Witnesses for soliciting funds for religious purposes in New Haven without a permit and playing before Roman Catholics in the same city a phonograph record attacking the Catholic Church. The Connecticut law under which conviction was obtained was ruled unconstitutional.

Newton Cantwell, and Jesse and Russell, his 16 and 18 year old sons, all ordained ministers of the sect, could not be convicted under a Connecticut law regulating the solicitation of funds, said justice Roberts, because the law was "a censorship of religion," and unconstitutional.

Jesse, who played the phonograph record, could not be convicted of breach of peace, the Justice added, because "however misguided others may think him," Jesse's conduct did not mean a violation of the "narrowly drawn" law.

"To condition the solicitation of aid for the perpetuation of religious views or systems upon a license the grant of which rests in the exercise of a determination by State authority as to what is a religious cause, is to lay a forbidden burden upon the exercise of liberty protected by the Constitution," Justice Roberts said.

"We find no assault or threatening of bodily harm, no truculent bearing, no intentional discourtesy, no personal abuse," Justice Roberts said of Jesse Cantwell. "On the contrary, we find only an effort to persuade a willing listener to buy a book or to contribute money in the interest of what Cantwell, however misguided others may think him, conceived to be true religion."

Throughout Justice Roberts's opinion ran the idea that, no matter how bitter religious differences might be, fundamental rights of individuals must be protected under the Constitution.

"In the realm of religious faith, and in that of political belief, sharp differences arise," the Justice stated.

> In both fields the tenets of one man may seem the rankest error to his neighbor.
>
> But people of this nation have ordained in the light of history, that, in spite of the probability of excesses and abuses, these liberties are, in the long view, essential to enlightened opinion and right conduct on the part of the citizens of a democracy.
>
> There are limits to the exercise of these liberties. The danger in these times from the coercive activities of those who in the delusion of racial or religious conceit would incite violence and breaches of the peace in order to deprive others of their equal right to the exercise of their liberties, is emphasized by events familiar to all. These and other transgressions of those limits the States appropriately may punish.

The Connecticut law, said Justice Roberts, deprived the Cantwells of their liberty without due process of law in contravention of the Fourteenth Amendment.

Supreme Court Ends Compulsion of Flag Salute

BY LEWIS WOOD | JUNE 15, 1943

WASHINGTON, JUNE 14 — In a reversal of the Gobitis decision of June, 1940, the Supreme Court held by 6 to 3 today that under the Bill of Rights public school children could not be compelled to salute the American flag if this ceremony conflicted with their religious beliefs.

The ruling was handed down while the nation was celebrating Flag Day in commemoration of the 164th anniversary of the Stars and Stripes.

It upheld a challenge by members of the sect of Jehovah's Witnesses to a flag-salute regulation issued by the West Virginia Board of Education.

In the Gobitis case the Witnesses brought a test against similar regulations of the Minersville, Pa., School District, but the Supreme Court then sustained the flag-salute order by 8 to 1.

PROTECTION BY CONSTITUTION

Writing the majority opinion in today's case, Justice Robert H. Jackson said:

> We think the action of the local authorities in compelling the flag salute and pledge transcends constitutional limitations on their power and invades the sphere of intellect and spirit which it is the purpose of the First Amendment to our Constitution to reserve from all official control.

The First Amendment protects freedom of religion, speech and the press, and right of assembly and petition.

Specifically overruling the Minersville and similar decisions, Justice Jackson also said:

To sustain the compulsory flag salute we are required to say that a Bill of Rights which guards the individual's right to speak his own mind left it open to public authorities to compel him to utter what is not in his mind.

Justices Owen J. Roberts, Stanley F. Reed and Felix Frankfurter all dissented, standing by their attitude in the Gobitis case, in which Harlan F. Stone, then an associate justice, alone opposed the compulsory flag salute.

Justices Hugo L. Black, William O. Douglas and Frank Murphy, who were in the majority in the Gobitis decision, written by Justice Frankfurter, switched in the new test. Justices Jackson and Wiley Rutledge were not members of the court in 1940.

SECT WINS OTHER CASES

Dealing with other controversies involving Jehovah's Witnesses, the Supreme Court today unanimously held invalid a Mississippi statute under which three members of the sect were convicted of sedition for disseminating teachings "tending to create an attitude of stubborn refusal to salute, honor and respect" the flag and the Federal Government.

Justice Roberts wrote this opinion, which was controlled by the West Virginia ruling. Following recent precedents, the jurists also arranged for dismissal of a case in which a Jehovah's Witness was convicted for selling literature in the District of Columbia.

In the West Virginia case Justice Jackson pointed out that children of the Jehovah's Witnesses, obeying a canon of the sect against worshiping an image, had been expelled from school and threatened with reformatory terms for refusal to salute the flag, while their parents had been prosecuted.

'RIGHTS OF THE INDIVIDUAL'

Asserting that the refusal of the children to participate in the ceremony did not interfere with or deny the rights of others to do so, Mr. Jackson continued:

The members of the Supreme Court, March 1943. Left to right, front row: Associate Justices Stanley F. Reed and Owen J. Roberts; Chief Justice Harlan Fiske Stone and Associate Justices Hugo Black and Felix Frankfurter. Back row: Associate Justices Robert H. Jackson, William O. Douglas, Frank Murphy and Wiley B. Ruthledge.

> *Nor is there any question in this case that their behavior is peaceful and orderly. The sole conflict is between authority and rights of the individual.*
> *The State asserts power to condition access to public education on making a prescribed sign and profession and at the same time to coerce attendance by punishing both parent and child. The latter stand on a right of self-determination in matters that touched individual opinion and personal attitude.*

Discussing the meaning of pledges and the flag salutes as symbols of an idea, Mr. Jackson remarked:

> *A person gets from a symbol the meaning he puts into it, and what is one man's comfort and inspiration is another's jest and scorn.*

More than ten years ago, Mr. Jackson recalled, Chief Justice Charles Evans Hughes:

... led this court in holding that the display of a red flag as a symbol of opposition to peaceful and legal means to organized government was protected by the free-speech guarantees of the Constitution.

Here it is the State that employs a flag as a symbol of adherence to government as presently organized," he went on. "It requires the individual to communicate by word and sign his acceptance of the political ideas it thus bespeaks.

Objection to this form of communication when coerced is an old one, well known to the framers of the Bill of Rights.

'FUTILITY' OF COMPULSION

Justice Jackson also said that there was a doubt whether Abraham Lincoln "would have thought that the strength of government to maintain itself would be impressively vindicated by our confirming power of the State to expel a handful of children from school."

Dwelling upon "the ultimate futility of such attempts to compel coherence," he added:

> To believe that patriotism will not flourish if patriotic ceremonies are voluntary and spontaneous instead of a compulsory routine is to make an unflattering estimate of the appeal of our institutions to free minds.
>
> If there is any fixed star in our constitutional constellation, it is that no official, high or petty, can prescribe what shall be orthodox in politics, nationalism, religion, or other matter of opinion, or force citizens to confess by word or act their faith therein.

DISSENT BY FRANKFURTER

In a separate dissent, Justice Frankfurter, a Jew, said that "one who belongs to the most vilified and persecuted minority in history is not likely to be insensible to the freedoms guaranteed by our Constitution."

He said that, were his "purely personal attitude relevant," he would whole-heartedly associate himself with "the general libertarian views in the Court's opinion, representing as they do the thought and action of a lifetime."

"But," he contended, "saluting the flag did not curb religious beliefs, and West Virginia had power to make the regulations without violating constitutional rights."

"It is self delusive to believe that the liberal spirit can be enforced by judicial invalidation of illiberal legislation," he stated.

Noting the existence of 250 religious denominations in the United States, he commented:

> *Certainly this court cannot be called upon to determine what claims of conscience should be recognized and what should be rejected as satisfying the 'religion' which the Constitution protects.*
>
> *I cannot bring my mind to believe that the 'liberty' secured by the Due Process Clause gives this court authority to deny to the State of West Virginia the attainment of that which we all recognize as a legitimate end — namely, the promotion of good citizenship, by employment of the means here chosen.*

Mr. Frankfurter pointed out that the flag salute had been five times previously before the Supreme Court, and that every justice — thirteen in all — who had participated "found no constitutional infirmity in what is now condemned."

Justices Roberts and Reed said in four lines that their judgment in the Gobitis decision was still correct. Justices Black and Douglas and Justice Murphy presented special concurrences with Justice Jackson.

With three major cases still on the calendar, the court announced another decision session for next Monday.

CHAPTER 4

The Separation of Church and State and More

The twentieth century brought with it new and different challenges to religious freedom. The classroom became the site of controversies regarding school prayer, public funds used in private religious schools and whether or not religious clubs could meet on campus. Limits on public monuments and displays of a religious nature met pushback by traditional Christians, and sex abuse scandals rocked the authority of the Catholic Church. The idea of separation of church and state became more pressing along with problems such as the AIDS epidemic, which struck the gay community first.

Religious Liberty Found Advancing

BY THE NEW YORK TIMES | JULY 3, 1939

THE AMERICAN CIVIL LIBERTIES UNION made public yesterday a survey entitled "Religious Liberty in the United States Today," which cited instances of restrictions imposed on various groups in many parts of the nation, but concluded that intolerance in this country is on the wane.

"On the whole, the restraints are slowly giving way to a larger freedom, but the united and uncompromising efforts of all those to whom religious liberty is a cherished ideal are necessary if it is to be maintained and extended," the survey said.

The forty-eight-page pamphlet said freedom of religion has not yet been read into the Fourteenth Amendment guaranteeing citizens against repressive State action, but held that future battles for religious liberty are likely to be waged chiefly in the Federal courts under its clauses.

The survey found that requirement of oaths of loyalty among teachers in twenty-one States and oaths in public office and the courts, the reading of the Protestant Bible in public schools, arbitrary enforcement of some Sunday laws, compulsory military service and discriminations against Catholics and Jews in a preponderantly Protestant country, gave rise to instances of intolerance.

Thirty-four religious leaders, educators and editors of various denominations in twelve States, have signed an introduction to the pamphlet.

Of greater public importance than discrimination in employment or public appointments, the pamphlet declared, "is the popular intolerance of the Protestant majority against Catholic and Jewish candidates for public elective offices."

The survey praised the work of the Federal Council of the Churches of Christ in America and the National Conference of Christians and Jews, composed of Protestants, Catholics and Jews, for promoting religious liberty.

High Court Backs State Right to Run Parochial Buses

BY LEWIS WOOD | FEB. 11, 1947

WASHINGTON, FEB. 10 — In a decision of far-flung interest the Supreme Court by 5 to 4 ruled today that New Jersey public school funds raised by taxation can be used to pay for transportation of children to Catholic parochial schools.

The controversy which the tribunal settled by this narrow margin revolved around the interpretation of the first amendment to the Constitution which forbids Congress to pass a law "respecting an establishment of religion, or prohibiting the free exercise thereof."

For the majority, Justice Hugo L. Black held that a New Jersey law permitting the payments amounts to religious or public benefit legislation and that no person may be barred from these benefits because of his religion. Justice Black was joined by Chief Justice Fred M. Vinson and Justices Stanley F. Reed, William O. Douglas and Frank Murphy.

EVERY FORM OF AID OPPOSED

The minority view expressed by Justice Wiley Rutledge, held that the First Amendment's purpose was to separate religious activity and civil authority by forbidding "every form" of public aid or support for religion. The dissent was shared by Justices Felix Frankfurter, Robert H. Jackson and Harold H. Burton.

In an independent objection, Justice Jackson, supported by Mr. Frankfurter, charged the majority with "giving the clock's hands a backward turn," because the prohibition against establishment of religion cannot be circumvented by a "subsidy, bonus or reimbursement."

The case, which required three opinions totaling seventy-three pages to dispose of, arose through a protest by Arch R. Everson, a taxpayer of Ewing Township, near Trenton in Mercer County. He contested the right of the township Board of Education to reimburse parents of Catholic children for transportation to the parochial schools on regular buses. A State court supported his protest, but was reversed by the New Jersey Court of Errors and Appeals, which was upheld by the Supreme Court today.

The Board of Education had authorized payment of $8,034 to be paid to parents of children for transportation to school, and for this $357.74 was reimbursed to the parents of the Catholic boys and girls.

Typical expressions from the three documents presented in the Supreme Court follow:

Majority, by Justice Black:

> New Jersey cannot exclude Catholics, Lutherans, Mohammedans, Baptists, Jews, Methodists, non-believers, Presbyterians, or the members of any other faith, because of their faith or lack of it. We must be careful, in protecting the citizens of New Jersey against State-established churches to be sure that we do not inadvertently prohibit New Jersey from extending its general State law benefits to all its citizens without regard to their religious belief.
>
> We cannot say that the First Amendment prohibits New Jersey from spending tax-raised funds to pay the bus fares of parochial schools as a part of a general program under which it pays the fares of pupils attending public and other schools. The First Amendment has erected a wall between church and State. That wall must be kept high and impregnable. We could not approve the slightest breach. New Jersey has not breached it here.

BURDEN OF TAXES CITED

Minority, by Justice Rutledge:

> No one conscious of religious values can be unsympathetic toward the burden which our constitutional separation puts on parents who desire religious instruction mixed with secular for their children. But if those feelings should prevail, there would be an end to our historic constitutional policy and command. No more unjust or discriminatory is it in fact to deny attendants at religious schools the cost of their transportation than it is to deny them tuitions, sustenance for their teachers, or any other educational expense which others receive at public cost.

Two great drives are constantly in motion to abridge, in the name of education, the complete division of religion and civil authority which our forefathers made. One is to introduce religious education and observances into the public schools. The other, to obtain public funds for the aid and support of various private religious schools. In my opinion both avenues were closed by the Constitution. Neither should be opened by this court.

Independent dissent by Justice Jackson, with Justice Frankfurter:

Catholic education is the rock on which the whole structure rests, and to render tax aid to its church school is indistinguishable to me from rendering the same aid to the church itself. The State cannot maintain a church and it can no more tax its citizens to furnish free carriage to those who attend a church. The prohibition against establishment of religion cannot be circumvented by a subsidy, bonus or reimbursement of expense to individuals for receiving religious instruction and indoctrination.

It (the church) does not leave the individual to pick up religion by chance. It relies on early and indelible indoctrination in the faith and order of the church by the word and example of persons consecrated to the task. The effect of the religious freedom amendment to our Constitution was to take every form of propagation of religion out of the realm of things which could be directly or indirectly be made public business and thereby be supported in whole or in part at taxpayers' expense.

In deciding this case, Justice Black dealt with two main attacks against the New Jersey practice. These were: 1. That the State law and Board of Education resolution take by taxation the private property of some persons and bestow it upon others for private use, thus violating the due process clause of the Fourteenth Amendment. 2. That the law and resolution force persons to pay taxes to help support Catholic schools, thus violating the First Amendment.

RIGHT PASS BENEFICIAL LAW

As to the first contention, the majority spokesman held that New Jersey must not be precluded from passing a law for the public benefit, and:

The fact that a State law, passed to satisfy a public need, coincides with the personal desires of the individuals most directly affected is certainly an inadequate reason for us to say that a legislature has erroneously appraised the public need.

Justice Rutledge, in his forty-seven-page dissent, described in detail the fight by Madison to separate church and state. New Jersey's action, he said, "exactly fit the type of exaction and the kind of evil at which Madison and Jefferson struck." Under the test they framed, "it cannot be said that the cost of transportation is no part of the cost of education or the religious instruction given."

The dissenting justice said any appropriation from the public treasury to pay the cost of transportation to Sunday School, or weekday classes at the church or parish house or to meetings of young people's religious societies such as the Y. M. C. A., Y. W. C. A., Y. M. H. A. or Epworth League "could not withstand the constitutional attack" brought against the New Jersey bus payments.

In his lengthy objection, Justice Rutledge also stated:

"The realm of religious training and belief remains as the amendment made it, the kingdom of the individual man and his God."

Justice Jackson in his separate opinion said he originally wished to join the majority. He said he had a sympathy "though not ideological" with Catholics who had to pay taxes for public schools and also felt it necessary to support schools for their own children. But, saying he had been forced to change his mind, he criticized the majority ruling.

"The undertones (of the majority) opinion," he added, "advocating complete and uncompromising separation of church from state seem utterly discordant with its conclusion yielding support to their comingling in education matters."

The Ewing Township Board of Education resolution authorized transportation of pupils from Ewing to "the Trenton and Pennington high schools and Catholic schools by way of public carrier." The Catholic schools were St. Mary's Cathedral high school, Trenton Catholic boys high school, St. Hedwig's parochial school and St. Francis school.

New York Church Leaders Divided Over Homosexual-Rights Measures

BY JOSEPH BERGER | FEB. 9, 1986

THE ISSUE OF homosexual-rights legislation has divided New York City's religious leaders and led to an uncommonly sharp exchange between John Cardinal O'Connor and Paul Moore Jr., the Episcopal Bishop of New York.

The conflict between the two religious leaders reflects a wider dispute within religion generally, over how literally the Bible should be interpreted and what attitudes one should adopt given some of the realities of contemporary society and the Bible's call for compassion.

"We are dealing with whether you take certain passages in the Bible literally or take the spirit of the Bible and apply it to our time," Bishop Moore has said.

Cardinal O'Connor, the Archbishop of New York, has assailed a bill pending in City Council that would forbid discrimination in housing and employment based on a person's "sexual orientation," which the bill defines as "heterosexuality, homosexuality or bisexuality."

He had also strongly opposed a mayoral directive, Executive Order 50, that prohibited discrimination against homosexuals by agencies, like those of the Roman Catholic Church, holding contracts with the city. That order was voided last year by the New York State Court of Appeals.

BISHOP ENDORSES BILL

Bishop Moore has strongly endorsed the City Council bill and supported the executive order, publicly criticizing Cardinal O'Connor for his stands. He has called the Cardinal "morally wrong" for initiating a lawsuit that successfully challenged the executive order. And last month, the Bishop said he "deeply regretted" the Cardinal's approach to the executive order.

"I think it is the more conservative approach, whether Jewish, Catholic or evangelical, against the more compassionate approach," he said.

"The funds which were being used are being raised from taxes from everybody, including the gay community," the Bishop said in a recent interview. "If we accept public funds then we must go along on the criteria by which public funds are administered. And I think trying to change the criteria is immoral. Anything that sets back the rights of an individual is not right."

Cardinal O'Connor, in an interview Tuesday, offered a cool response to the Bishop's remarks. "The Bishop feels the need to make public comments about my sense of morality," the Cardinal said. "I don't feel the same need. I can only assume he's following his conscience."

"My inclination is not to call people I think are wrong immoral," he said.

CHURCH GROUPS' ATTITUDES

The Old and New Testaments contain at least five passages condemning homosexual behavior. The Roman Catholic Church asserts that having homosexual inclinations is morally neutral, while acting on those inclinations is sinful. Conservative Protestants essentially take the Biblical passages literally, and more liberal Protestant denominations emphasize the Bible's call for compassion.

A few liberal denominations have taken public stands opposing discrimination against homosexuals in hiring and housing. Although Bishop Moore supports the ordination of homosexuals, the Episcopal Church has refused to pass a forceful statement supporting that idea. Almost every sect endorses marriage between men and women as the moral ideal.

The range in Jewish thought is also wide. Orthodox and Conservative Jews in varying degrees condemn homosexuality, while Reform Judaism believes in equal rights for homosexuals, including ordination as rabbis.

The Cardinal argues that the Roman Catholic Church does not discriminate against homosexuals and is prepared to employ people who have a homosexual orientation or have practiced homosexuality in the past.

'HUMAN WEAKNESS'

"I am prepared to consider such people for employment because it is a human weakness just as I would employ someone who practiced illicit heterosexual behavior in the past," Cardinal O'Connor said. "But I cannot accept the premise that anyone must engage in homosexual behavior any more than I must accept that someone must engage in heterosexual behavior."

Moreover, the Cardinal argues that support of the City Council bill would place the church in the position of sanctioning homosexuality. Last week, he and Bishop Francis J. Mugavero of the Roman Catholic Diocese of Brooklyn issued a joint statement condemning the City Council bill for placing homosexuality and bisexuality on an equal footing with heterosexuality.

"Such a result would seriously undermine the moral education and values of our youth and the stability of families in our society," the statement said.

Bishop Moore has for years supported bills banning discrimination against homosexuals, testifying in favor of the bills at legislative hearings. "The principle here is that a person should not be discriminated against because of something he or she cannot help," the Bishop said. "If I'm black, a woman or old, or made gay, I should not be discriminated against."

BIAS BECAUSE OF AIDS CITED

The need for antidiscrimination legislation, he said, is more imperative than ever because men thought to be homosexual are increasingly facing discrimination in hiring and housing as a result of the public fears caused by the epidemic of AIDS, or acquired immune deficiency syndrome.

The Cardinal says current laws protect people from discrimination when the reasons for discrimination are not related to job qualifications or performance. What greatly worries him, he said, is that the new bill could lead to a civic sanctioning of homosexual marriages and to a requirement that teachers in sex-education classes espouse homosexuality as a morally valid sexual option.

Bishop Moore has pointed out that the new City Council bill excluded religious groups from its strictures. The Cardinal argued that his experience during the period that Executive Order 50 was in effect led him to believe that city agencies could still harass church groups.

Excerpts From Decision
on Separation of Church and State

SPECIAL TO THE NEW YORK TIMES | JUNE 30, 1988

WASHINGTON, JUNE 29 — Following are excerpts from the Supreme Court's decision today upholding a Federal law providing, with an important qualification, money to religious organizations to counsel teen-age girls to abstain from sex and to avoid abortion. Chief Justice William H. Rehnquist wrote the opinion, joined by Justices Byron R. White, Antonin Scalia and Anthony M. Kennedy. Justice Sandra Day O'Connor filed a separate opinion concurring in the judgment.

Justice Harry A. Blackmun dissented, joined by Justices William J. Brennan Jr., Thurgood Marshall and John Paul Stevens.

FROM THE OPINION
By Justice Rehnquist

The Adolescent Family Life Act was passed by Congress in 1981 in response to the "severe adverse health, social, and economic consequences" that often follow pregnancy and childbirth among unmarried adolescents. Like its predecessor, the Adolescent Health Services and Pregnancy Prevention and Care Act of 1978, the A.F.L.A. is essentially a scheme for providing grants to public or nonprofit private organizations or agencies "for services and research in the area of premarital adolescent sexual relations and pregnancy."

These grants are intended to serve several purposes, including the promotion of "self-discipline and other prudent approaches to the problem of adolescent premarital sexual relations," the promotion of adoption as an alternative for adolescent parents, the establishment of new approaches to the delivery of care services for pregnant adolescents, and the support of research and demonstration projects "concerning the social causes and consequences of adolescent premarital sexual relations, contraceptive use, pregnancy, and child rearing."

144 RELIGIOUS FREEDOM

141 Grants Since 1981

Since 1981, when the A.F.L.A. was adopted, the Secretary has received 1,088 grant applications and awarded 141 grants. Funding has gone to a wide variety of recipients, including state and local health agencies, private hospitals, community health associations, privately operated health care centers, and community and charitable organizations. It is undisputed that a number of grantees or subgrantees were organizations with institutional ties to religious denominations.

In 1983, this lawsuit against the Secretary was filed in the United States District Court for the District of Columbia by appellees, a group of Federal taxpayers, clergymen, and the American Jewish Congress. Seeking both declaratory and injunctive relief, appellees challenged the constitutionality of the A.F.L.A. on the grounds that on its face and as applied, the statute violates the religion clauses of the First Amendment.

Following cross-motions for summary judgment, the District Court held for appellees and delcared that the A.F.L.A. was invalid both on its face and as applied "insofar as religious organizations are involved in carrying out the programs and purposes of the Act."

2 'On Its Face' Tests

There are two ways in which the statute, considered "on its face," might be said to have the impermissible primary effect of advancing religion. First, it can be argued that the A.F.L.A. advances religion by expressly recognizing that "religious organizations have a role to play" in addressing the problems associated with teen-age sexuality.

In this view, even if no religious institution receives aid or funding pursuant to the A.F.L.A., the statute is invalid under the Establishment Clause because, among other things, it expressly enlists the involvement of religiously affiliated organizations in the Federally subsidized programs, it endorses religious solutions to the problems addressed by the Act, or it creates symbolic ties between church and state.

Secondly, it can be argued that the A.F.L.A. is invalid on its face because it allows religiously affiliated organizations to participate as grantees or subgrantees in A.F.L.A. programs. From this standpoint, the Act is invalid because it authorizes direct Federal funding of religious organizations which, given the A.F.L.A.'s educational function and the fact that the A.F.L.A.'s "viewpoint" may coincide with the grantee's "viewpoint" on sexual matters, will result unavoidably in the impermissible "inculcation" of religious beliefs in the context of a Federally funded program … .

This brings us to the second grounds for objecting to the A.F.L.A.: the fact that it allows religious institutions to participate as recipients of Federal funds. The A.F.L.A. defines an "eligible grant recipient" as a "public or nonprofit private organization or agency" [that] demonstrates the capability of providing the requisite services. As this provision would indicate, a fairly wide spectrum of organizations is eligible to apply for and receive funding under the Act, and nothing on the face of the Act suggests the A.F.L.A. is anything but neutral with respect to the grantee's status as a sectarian or purely secular institution. …

We have concluded that the statute has a valid secular purpose, does not have the primary effect of advancing religion, and does not create an excessive entanglement of church and state. We note that the statute does not violate the Establishment Clause and is consistent with the conclusion Congress reached in the course of its deliberations on the A.F.L.A.

It seems to us that the District Court did not follow the proper approach in assessing appellees' claim that the Secretary is making grants under the Act that violate the Establishment Clause of the First Amendment.

Although the District Court stated several times that A.F.L.A. aid had been given to religious organizations that were "pervasively sectarian," it did not identify which grantees it was referring to, nor did it discuss with any particularity the aspects of those organizations which in its view warranted classification as "pervasively sectarian."

The District Court did identify certain instances in which it felt A.F.L.A. funds were used for constitutionally improper purposes, but in our view the court did not adequately design its remedy to address the specific problems it found in the Secretary's administration of the statute.

… We feel that this case should be remanded to the District Court for consideration of the evidence presented by appellees insofar as it sheds light on the manner in which the statute is presently being administered. It is the latter inquiry to which the Court must direct itself on remand.

In particular, it will be open to appellees on remand to show that A.F.L.A. aid is flowing to grantees that can be considered "pervasively sectarian" religious institutions … It is not enough to show that the recipient of a challenged grant is affiliated with a religious institution or that it is "religiously inspired."

FROM THE DISSENT
By Justice Blackmun

The A.F.L.A., without a doubt, endorses religion. Because of its expressed solicitude for the participation of religious organizations in all A.F.L.A. programs in one form or another, the statute creates a symbolic and real partnership between the clergy and the fisc in addressing a problem with substantial religious overtones.

Given the delicate subject matter and the impressionable audience, the risk that the A.F.L.A. will convey a message of Government endorsement of religion is overwhelming. The statutory language and the extensive record established in the District Court make clear that the problem lies in the statute and its systematically unconstitutional operation, and not merely in isolated instances of misapplication. I therefore would find the statute unconstitutional without remanding to the District Court.

I trust, however, that after all its labors thus far, the District Court will not grow weary prematurely and read into the Court's decision a suggestion that the A.F.L.A. has been constitutionally implemented by the Government, for the majority deliberately eschews any review of the facts. After such further proceedings as are now to be deemed appropriate, and after the District Court enters findings of fact on the basis of the testimony and documents entered into evidence, it may well decide, as I would today, that the A.F.L.A. as a whole indeed has been unconstitutionally applied.

Arab Girls' Veils at Issue in France

BY YOUSSEF M. IBRAHIM | NOV. 12, 1989

PARIS, NOV. 11 — The question of whether girls may wear Iranian-style veils to school has become a heated political controversy in this most secular of Western European countries.

It started about a month ago, when a principal told three Muslim teen-agers that they could not attend high school in Creil, a suburb of Paris, if they insisted on wearing the enveloping head cover associated with the most conservative Muslim societies.

The confrontation set off a furious debate over civil rights and the separation of church and state in France, which has a century-old tradition of secularism in public schools. The debate has resulted in public spectacles like the appearance of two deputies at the National Assembly in women's scarves and demonstrations in the streets of Paris.

Education Minister Lionel Jospin decided two weeks ago that Muslim fundamentalist girls should be "persuaded" to take off their veils in class. But if they refused, he said, they should not be denied access to the classroom, since this would constitute a form of religious discrimination.

SOME SEE VEIL AS HUMILIATING

His views were vigorously rejected by France's teachers, many members of his own Socialist Party, and virtually all of the opposition, who argued that secularism and equal treatment of pupils were basic principles of France's public educational system.

Wearing a veil creates a religious distinction among pupils, they said. Some also denounced the veil as a humiliating form of dress for women.

The issue has deeply divided France's progressive left. Some argue that the veil poses no problem because a small fundamentalist minority cannot threaten a secular society of 55 million people. Others see the veil as an insult to the principle of women's emancipation, a cause, they say, that has long been settled in France and should not be fought again.

Gisèle Halimi, a prominent lawyer and a founding member of France's anti-racist organization, S.O.S.-Racism, resigned from the group last week when it asserted that Muslim women should be allowed to wear the veil if they wished.

"It is a sign of imprisonment that considers women to be subhumans under the law of Islam," she said.

EVEN CABINET IS DIVIDED

The French teachers' union has threatened a strike over the issue. Politicians, even those within the Socialist Government of Prime Minister Michel Rocard, are so divided on the veil that Mr. Rocard referred the question a week ago to the highest council of government, the Council of State, for a judgment.

"The past few weeks have brought into question the need to have a secular system which is at once faithful to the principles of tolerance and to those of progress and emancipation," said Mr. Rocard, whose Government has supported policies favorable to immigrant communities.

For France and much of Western Europe, where an estimated 10 million to 11 million Muslims now live, the question involves more than the separation of church and state. As the newspaper Le Monde put it, "It could conclude with a grand debate over immigration."

The veil controversy points to growing social conflict from the difficulties of integrating conservative Muslim immigrants, many of whom arrived to fill a demand for cheap labor, into liberal West European societies. Many of those immigrants have settled in France, West Germany and Belgium.

IMMIGRATION AND RACISM

Arabs in France have become particular targets of racism. Over the last few years, the incidents have multiplied, with Muslim places of worship destroyed or desecrated and North African immigrants attacked.

The teen-age girls who touched off the crisis are 14-year-old Leila and 13-year-old Fatima Achaboun, daughters of a devout Moroccan immigrant who is employed at an automobile body shop, and 14-year-old Samira Saeedani, whose unemployed Tunisian father was once a municipal worker and spends his time teaching Islam in his neighborhood.

Like many Muslim children here, the girls are part of a generation of Arabs born in France whose outlook mixes West and East. Along with the veil, many of the girls wear blue jeans.

Beyond the Muslim issue, there are Jews and Christians who also seek greater freedom to practice their religion in the public schools.

'CHASING GOD OUT OF PUBLIC'

Many Jewish families keep their children at home on Saturdays to observe the Sabbath, although French schoolchildren normally attend classes on Saturday for a half day. Some Jewish families would like their children to attend school in yarmulkes, which are not permitted.

Some Catholics also are anxious. "We must not, under the pretext of secularism, chase God out of every public expression in society," the Archbishop of Lyons, Albert Cardinal Decourtray, said recently.

Ernest Chenières, the principal of the school in Creil, conceded last week that he could not decide on the issue's merits as an administrator.

"Since there is in France and in Europe an alien religious current to the existing traditions that is beginning, by its very nature, to pose questions about our current values," he said, "it is important that the marriage contract between our republican, secular societies and these religious and political forces representing Islam be clarified."

A Church-State Conflict Arises Over AIDS Care

BY BRUCE LAMBERT | FEB. 23, 1990

A CLASH BETWEEN Roman Catholic officials and New York State over the counseling of AIDS patients is jeopardizing AIDS care at the church's hospitals and nursing homes, which are major providers of such services in New York City, church and state leaders say.

The Catholic institutions are under attack for religious prohibitions against the counseling of patients on a number of matters: using condoms or engaging in safe sex practices, using clean needles if the AIDS patient is an intravenous drug user, and using contraception or resorting to abortion if the patient is in peril of giving birth to a baby with AIDS.

Today the issue formally goes before the State Public Health Council. The New York Archdiocese seeks the council's approval for two new publicly financed AIDS nursing homes of 100 beds each at 308-12 East 8th Street and 99th Street near Second Avenue in Manhattan.

The broader implication is that millions of dollars in public funds and medical care for thousands of patients at Catholic institutions are at stake.

Objections to church policies raised by more than a dozen AIDS, civil liberties and other advocacy organizations forced the council to delay its vote last month.

The church's critics say theological restrictions bar patients from getting complete, medically correct information to prevent the spread of AIDS, resulting in more people becoming infected and sick and dying. They accuse the state of dodging the issue by failing its regulatory duty to require hospitals to give proper counseling.

The Archbishop of New York, John Cardinal O'Connor, preaches abstinence from sex and drugs as the only sure way to prevent infection. He says alternative preventive measures like engaging in safe

The Catholic Church's stand on AIDS has created a conflict over church-state issues that has jeopardized AIDS care at Catholic hospitals and nursing homes. John Cardinal O'Connor preaches abstinence from sex and drugs as the only sure way to prevent infection.

sex are morally sinful and medically dangerous; he says these practices will actually increase the spread of AIDS.

The Cardinal wrote yesterday: "Should funding be cut off because of our refusal to instruct in condoms, we will be forced to close our doors to such critically ill persons with AIDS." In an interview, he asked: "What will happen? Who's going to take care of those people?"

MUTUAL SELF-INTERESTS

Thomas B. Stoddard, executive director of the Lambda Legal Defense Fund, a gay rights organization that opposes the church's stand, said: "This is a classic church-state issue. There's an unhealthy if not unconstitutional entanglement between New York State and the Catholic hierarchy."

Behind the clash of principles, the church and state are bound by powerful mutual interests.

The state desperately needs the Catholic-operated beds, because the health-care system is suffering unprecedented overcrowding. At the same time, the church depends on public subsidies to run its services.

"We need this kind of commitment, and we need it badly," Gov. Mario M. Cuomo said last month in a news conference with the Cardinal announcing the nursing homes.

'WE DON'T HAVE THE MONEY'

The Cardinal said: "The church is critically strapped in its finances. We just cannot find the money without governmental support, city support, state support — to take care of the endless numbers of persons with AIDS. We want to do it; we don't have the money."

About 350 AIDS patients are housed in hospitals run by the New York Archdiocese and the Brooklyn Diocese and in one nursing home operated by the church, making up a sixth of all such AIDS care in the city. Catholic hospital clinics also serve thousands more outpatients who have AIDS infection or illness or who are at risk of getting the AIDS virus.

The state's role is to regulate health care, help pay for Medicaid patients and sometimes finance nursing homes. State officials concede they have not stressed monitoring of AIDS information at hospitals but said they intend to do more.

Neither has the church universally enforced its doctrine, medical sources said. They said staff members often ignore official pronouncements and quietly inform patients about sex practices and drug precautions frowned on by the church.

A POLICY CONTRADICTION?

A potential compromise has come in a letter to the state from John F. Keane, an Archdiocesean nursing home official. The letter offered to provide "accurate" and "comprenhensive" AIDS information in the nursing homes, and to refer patients to outside agencies for condoms and contraceptive and abortion services.

That plan appears to contradict the Cardinal's policy, which holds that as long as a patient is under the church's care, "then we feel we must adhere to our institutional conscience" and abide by its doctrines.

The State Health Department's AIDS Institute concluded "this issue remains unresolved." The institute, headed by Dr. Nicholas Rango, has requested authorization to monitor the AIDS counseling and, if necessary, intercede and run the program directly. But a nursing home aide has criticized that proposal.

Anti-Abortion Bill in Idaho Takes Aim at Landmark Case

BY TIMOTHY EGAN | MARCH 22, 1990

BOISE, IDAHO, MARCH 21 — The Idaho Legislature is expected to approve an abortion bill on Thursday that is specifically intended to persuade a pivotal Supreme Court Justice to overturn the landmark ruling that legalized abortion nationwide.

The proposed legislation, described by both supporters and opponents as the most restrictive in any state, is aimed at the perceived objections of Justice Sandra Day O'Connor, who is considered a swing vote as the divided Court takes up cases challenging the 1973 ruling in Roe v. Wade.

The National Right to Life Committee considers Idaho its last and best hope this year to pass what it considers its model anti-abortion legislation. It has tried, and failed, to pass similar bills in several legislatures, including in such conservative states as Alabama and Utah.

CRUCIAL VOTE OF JUSTICE

"What we're after here is Sandra Day O'Connor," said Brian Johnston, the Western regional director of the anti-abortion group. "We know Justice O'Connor wants to overturn Roe v. Wade. We just have to give her something she's comfortable with."

Although Justice O'Connor has voted to uphold abortion restrictions in every case she has heard on the Supreme Court, her written opinions have stopped short of an unambiguous declaration that Roe v. Wade should be overturned. As a result, some people believe that she would be less likely than the other conservatives on the Court to uphold stringent criminal penalties on abortion.

The abortion opponents who drafted the Idaho legislation have sought to address this by placing the criminal penalties on the doctors rather than women having an abortion.

Opponents of the bill, which has already passed the Idaho House, concede that they do not have the votes to defeat it in the Senate.

The legislation would allow doctors to end a pregnancy only in these situations:

• In cases of rape, if the victim reported the crime to the authorities within seven days.

• In cases of incest, if the victim was under 18 years old and reported the incest to the authorities sometime before the abortion.

• In cases of "profound" fetal deformity in the judgment of a doctor.

• In cases where a doctor believes that the physical health of the woman would be threatened by completing the pregnancy. The bill includes no provisions dealing with the woman's mental health.

FINES OF $10,000

Doctors who violate major provisions of the measure would face civil fines up to $10,000 and civil lawsuits by the father of the fetus or anyone else with standing in the case, like a parent of a minor child and a prosecuting attorney.

There would be no penalties for the woman, unless she tried to abort her own fetus, in which case she would face a $10,000 fine.

Both sides say that, based on a review of abortions done in Idaho, about 95 percent of them would now be illegal. About 1,650 abortions are performed each year in the state.

SHIFTING ONUS TO DOCTORS

By putting the onus on doctors to decide who meets these requirements, abortion opponents say they hope to satisfy what they see as Justice O'Connor's main objection to abortion restrictions: making the woman criminally liable if she has an abortion. In essence, the Idaho legislation shifts that burden entirely to doctors.

Gov. Cecil D. Andrus, a Democrat who has just announced his decision to run for a fourth term, has not said whether he will sign the bill. But he has repeatedly expressed opposition to abortion, a position that he reiterated this week.

Even if Governor Andrus signs the bill, the measure could face a statewide vote of the people in November. In Idaho, as elsewhere in the West, voter-initiated referendums can set or overturn laws passed by the legislature. People are already gathering signatures on petitions to put the issue on the ballot.

With the crucial vote here set for Thursday in the State Senate, lobbyists for both sides have converged on this desert capitol in the Snake River basin, where a heavily Mormon population that opposes abortion is at odds with people who have moved here from California and elsewhere.

The abortion debate in the Idaho legislature comes only days after the territorial legislature in Guam passed a law that explicitly challenges that constitutional right to abortion that was established in Roe v. Wade. Because Guam and other territories are under the jurisdiction of the United States court system, a case could go from the District Court there to the Court of Appeals for the Ninth Circuit, in San Francisco, and on to the Supreme Court.

The American Civil Liberties Union plans to challenge the bill as soon as it becomes law, setting up a court fight that could last up to three years and possibly suspend the restrictions until the legal issues are resolved.

'AN IMPOSSIBLE SITUATION'

"What this will do is force the women of Idaho into back-alley abortions or into trying something themselves," said Jack Van Valkenburgh, a lobbyist for the civil liberties group here. "Because the burden of proof will be on the doctor to assure that the pregnancy was caused by rape or incest, it sets up an impossible situation for medical professionals."

Mr. Van Valkenburgh said that under the Idaho proposal a man who had committed "date rape," a term describing sexual assault by an acquaintance, could conceivably force the woman to carry the child.

"It's clearly unconstitutional," said State Senator Joyce McRoberts, a Republican. "Abortion is just too personal an issue to allow one legislative body to decide on it."

Mrs. McRoberts said the bill was an attempt to impose the philosophy of the Mormon Church, which dominates much of southern Idaho, on all citizens of the state.

"I don't like the fact that this bill was written and is being pushed so heavily by outsiders," she said, referring to national anti-abortion groups and the Church of Jesus Christ of Latter-day Saints. "Why should our laws be somebody else's vehicle? Maybe what we should do is eliminate the men from voting on this, since they seem to be the ones most in favor of it."

But State Senator Michael D. Crapo, the president pro-tem of the Senate, who identified himself as a devout Mormon, said the church had nothing to do with the legislation.

"I've never received a phone call from the church leadership telling me how to vote," Mr. Crapo said. "The idea that this is imposing someone's religious belief is absurd."

Mr. Crapo said those in favor of the legislation had a 4-vote lead in the 42-member upper chamber. The sentiment among political leaders here against abortion is a reflection of this state's conservative attitude, he said.

Another Senator, Mary Hartung, also a Republican, said she was uncertain how she would vote until today, when mail and phone calls from her constituents helped persuade her to favor the restrictive bill.

Those favoring abortion rights have predicted severe health consequences for women if the restrictive measure passes.

But Mrs. Hartung said it would be just as easy for an Idaho woman to get an abortion in neighboring Washington, Oregon or

Montana, where polls have shown a majority preference for legalized abortion.

Since last summer, when a Supreme Court ruling in a Missouri case allowed states to limit access to abortions, several states have taken action to restrict abortions. The most stringent of those measures was passed in Pennsylvania, but a Federal judge blocked major provisions of that legislation from taking effect. Cases from Minnesota and Ohio are expected to be decided this spring by the Supreme Court, but like the Missouri law, they do not challenge the basic premise of Roe v. Wade.

Use of Drugs in Religious Rituals Can Be Prosecuted, Justices Rule

BY LINDA GREENHOUSE | APRIL 18, 1990

WASHINGTON, APRIL 17 — The Supreme Court ruled today that governments may prosecute those who use illegal drugs as part of religious rituals. It said such prosecutions were not a violation of the constitutional guarantee of religious freedom.

By a vote of 6 to 3, the Court refused to grant two men who are members of an American Indian church a religious exemption from an Oregon law that makes it a crime to possess or use peyote.

The decision, written by Justice Antonin Scalia, has broader implications for the Court's approach to resolving the conflicts that occur with some frequency between individual religious practice and generally applicable government policies.

The ruling overturned a decision by the Oregon Supreme Court that the First Amendment's protection for the "free exercise" of religion required an exemption in state law for the sacramental use of peyote.

A 'DESIRABLE' EXEMPTION

Oregon had not sought to prosecute the two men, who used peyote in the rituals of the Native American Church. Rather, the state's employment division refused to pay the men unemployment benefits after they were dismissed from their jobs for using peyote. The state agency said the criminal status of peyote use rendered the men ineligible for the benefits.

Peyote, a cactus that contains the hallucinogenic substance mescaline, has been used for centuries in Indian religious ceremonies. Federal law and the laws of 23 states, including many with substantial Indian populations, exempt the sacramental use of peyote from criminal penalties.

Justice Scalia said such an exemption was permissible, even "desirable," as a choice for legislators to make. But, he added, "the First Amendment's protection of religious liberty does not require this."

He noted that the Court ruled more than a century ago that Mormons could be prosecuted for polygamy even though their religion incorporated it. "We have never held that an individual's religious beliefs excuse him from compliance with an otherwise valid law prohibiting conduct that the State is free to regulate," he said.

"It may fairly be said that leaving accommodation to the political process will place at a relative disadvantage those religious practices that are not widely engaged in," Justice Scalia said, "but that unavoidable consequence of democratic government must be preferred to a system in which each conscience is a law unto itself."

A generally applicable law or regulation that places an incidental burden on religious practice is constitutional, Justice Scalia said, unless it is "specifically directed" at a religious act. As an example, he said, a law prohibiting "bowing down before a golden calf" would "doubtless be unconstitutional."

The majority's analysis drew strong dissents, not only from the three Justices who said the Constitution required an exemption for sacramental peyote use, but also from Justice Sandra Day O'Connor, who agreed with the outcome of the case but differed sharply with Justice Scalia's approach.

The three Justices who disagreed with the outcome as well as the approach were Thurgood Marshall, Harry A. Blackmun and William J. Brennan Jr. In her opinion concurring only in the result of the case, Justice O'Connor called the majority opinion "incompatible with our nation's fundamental commitment to individual religious liberty."

'VITALITY' OF FIRST AMENDMENT

She added: "If the First Amendment is to have any vitality, it ought not be construed to cover only the extreme and hypothetical situation in which a state directly targets a religious practice," she said.

"The essence of a free exercise claim," she said, "is relief from a burden imposed by government on religious practices or beliefs, whether the burden is imposed directly through laws that prohibit or compel specific religious practices, or indirectly through laws that, in effect, make abandonment of one's own religious or conformity to the religious beliefs of others the price of an equal place in the civil community.

"The history of our free-exercise doctrine amply demonstrates the harsh impact majoritarian rule has had on unpopular or emerging religious groups such as the Jehovah's Witnesses and the Amish."

In addition to filing their own dissenting opinion, Justices Blackmun, Marshall and Brennan signed much of Justice O'Connor's opinion. All four agreed that the Government must be required to justify a burden on religious practice by demonstrating that it served a "compelling state interest."

Justice O'Connor concluded that Oregon could have met that test in this case because of the state's compelling interest in curbing drug use. The three others concluded that the state's interest was not sufficiently compelling.

Justice Scalia's majority opinion rejected the "compelling state interest" test, saying it would "open the prospect of constitutionally required religious exemptions from civic obligations of almost every conceivable kind."

He said: "We cannot afford the luxury of deeming presumptively invalid, as applied to a religious objector, every regulation of conduct that does not protect an interest of the highest order."

The majority opinion, Employment Division v. Smith, No. 88-1213, was joined by Chief Justice William H. Rehnquist and Justices Byron R. White, John Paul Stevens and Anthony M. Kennedy.

High Court Rules Religious Clubs Can Meet in Public High Schools

BY LINDA GREENHOUSE | JUNE 5, 1990

WASHINGTON, JUNE 4 — The Supreme Court today upheld a 1984 Federal law that requires public high schools to allow students' religious and political clubs to meet on the same basis as other extracurricular activities.

A high school need not permit any student activities not related to the curriculum, Justice Sandra Day O'Connor said in the opinion. But she said that if it does, the school is bound by the Equal Access Act not to discriminate against any student group on the basis of its religious, philosophical or political viewpoint.

The decision, in a case from a public school district in Omaha, upheld a ruling last year by the United States Court of Appeals for the Eighth Circuit, in St. Louis. A group of Omaha high school students led by Bridget Mergens Mayhew, then a senior at Westside High School, successfully sued the school district in 1985 after being denied official recognition for a Christian Bible club.

UNDERCOVER ROLE UPHELD

In another decision today overturning an appellate ruling, the Court ruled that a law-enforcement officer can pose as a prison inmate and elicit a confession from an actual inmate even though the officer gives no Miranda warning about the inmate's constitutional rights.

The Omaha case was the latest battle over the place of religion in the public schools, and today's decision could affect other cases.

In Buffalo, a student Bible group won temporary permission from a judge to meet at a high school after school officials barred them. In Renton, Wash., the United States Court of Appeals for the Ninth Circuit struck down the Equal Access Act on the basis of a 1989 appeal by high school students who wanted to start a Bible study club.

Bridget Mergens Mayhew, who sued after school officials blocked formation of a Bible club.

"There are a lot of schools waiting for this decision," said Virginia Roach, project director for the National Association of State Boards of Education.

By a vote of 8-to-1, the Justices today rejected arguments that the Equal Access Act breached the constitutionally required separation between church and state. But the Court's constitutional analysis was splintered. Three separate opinions, none commanding a majority, supported the result. The eight Justices agreed, however, that the Federal law was not an unconstitutional "establishment of religion" by the Government.

The only dissenter was Justice John Paul Stevens, who said the Court had interpreted the Federal law in a way that left too little discretion to local school districts.

'STUDENTS ARE MATURE ENOUGH'

In essence, today's decision was an extension of a 1981 Supreme Court ruling, Widmar v. Vincent, in which the Court held that public universities had to permit student religious groups to meet on the same terms afforded other student organizations. That ruling suggested, without deciding, that the analysis might be different for younger, more impressionable students below the college level.

In her opinion today, Justice O'Connor said: "We think the logic of Widmar applies with equal force to the Equal Access Act. We think that secondary school students are mature enough and are likely to understand that a school does not endorse or support student speech that it merely permits on a nondiscriminatory basis."

She went on, "There is a crucial difference between *government* speech endorsing religion, which the establishment clause forbids, and private speech endorsing religion, which the free speech and free exercise clauses protect." Those three clauses are in the First Amendment to the Constitution.

The case, Westside Community Board of Education v. Mergens, No. 88-1597, was one of the more politically charged of the Court's term, now in its final month. The Equal Access Act was a long-sought goal of the religious right after the defeat of earlier efforts to bring prayer back to public school classrooms. The law was strongly supported in Congress by the Reagan Administration and in the Supreme Court by the Bush Administration.

REACTION TO THE RULING

Many friend-of-the-Court briefs were filed. A number of Jewish groups, including the American Jewish Congress, the American Jewish Committee and the Anti-Defamation League of B'nai B'rith, urged the Court to strike down the law, as did the American Civil Liberties Union and People for the American Way. But a number of Protestant and Catholic groups filed briefs supporting the law.

Burton S. Levinson, chairman of the Anti-Defamation League, said today that the ruling was "troubling because it sanctions the use of public school facilities to advance religion in violation of the First Amendment."

Mrs. Mayhew, now 23 years old, told The Associated Press today that the decision sent a clear message to schools that they could not discriminate against religion. "It's a source of strength to be able to share your faith and share what you believe," she said. "I think it's a very important part of that age because you're a kid and you've got all these things coming at you."

TYING ACTIVITIES TO CURRICULUM

The Equal Access Act applies to "any public secondary school which receives Federal financial assistance and which has a limited open forum." Virtually all public schools receive some Federal money. Justice O'Connor noted that high schools could remove themselves from the law by refusing Federal money, although she added that "this may be an unrealistic option."

The Act says that a school has a "limited open forum" if it permits at least one "noncurriculum related" student group to meet on the premises.

The school district argued that all 30 of the student organizations at the high school, including the chess club and the scuba diving club, were related to the curriculum, and that the school was therefore not an open forum under the law.

But the Court rejected this argument in a section of Justice O'Connor's opinion that five other Justices joined. She said that Congress meant "to provide a low threshold for triggering the Act's requirements" and that a school would be covered unless all student activities were tied directly to the curriculum. For example, she said, participation in a band or orchestra would be directly related to the curriculum if it resulted in academic credit.

CLARIFYING SCHOOL'S POSITION

In a separate concurring opinion, Justices Thurgood Marshall and William J. Brennan Jr. said that depending on the context, the majority's approach to the open forum question could pose a danger under the Establishment Clause.

They said that schools that already permit organizations with distinct or controversial viewpoints could more readily absorb a religious club than a school in which only a few student clubs engaged in advocacy. In that situation, the two Justices said, the school "must fully dissociate itself" from a religious club to make clear that it was not sponsoring or endorsing the club's goals.

Justice O'Connor's opinion was joined in full by Chief Justice William H. Rehnquist and by Justices Byron R. White and Harry A. Blackmun. Justices Anthony M. Kennedy and Antonin Scalia filed a separate concurring opinion in which they said that recognition of religious clubs was constitutional as long as no student was coerced to participate.

CHAPTER 5

Twenty-First Century Issues

Issues of religious freedom continue to evolve in the new millennium. Conflicts have arisen about religious monuments in government spaces. Republican president Donald Trump claimed that a travel ban against Muslim immigrants was not based on their Islamic faith. State and federal judges and courts sometimes supported Trump's position and sometimes contradicted it. Evangelical Christianity's disapproval of the gay lifestyle resulted in a Supreme Court battle over the question of when a person's religious liberty superseded others' rights to live as they please.

Voucher Ruling Seen as Further Narrowing Church-State Division

BY LAURIE GOODSTEIN | JUNE 28, 2002

HAVING WON THE BATTLE to convince the Supreme Court that government vouchers for religious schools are constitutional, religious advocates are now planning to push efforts to channel an increasing amount of public money into other religious programs, including charities and social services, hospitals and even foreign aid missions.

The Cleveland school voucher program that the Supreme Court upheld yesterday provides a particularly useful model for religious organizations because it did not finance parochial schools directly, but instead gave vouchers worth $2,500 each to parents, who could choose to spend them at those schools.

"If you can have vouchers for parochial school children, you can surely have vouchers for adults who need substance abuse treatment and want to get that treatment from a religious program," said Kevin J. Hasson, president of the Becket Fund for Religious Liberty, a legal advocacy group that often represents religious groups.

The decision comes at a time when the government is already moving to lift the barriers to using tax money for religious programs. This was the concept behind both the "charitable choice" provisions of the 1996 welfare reform package and President Bush's "faith-based initiative," a cornerstone of his election campaign. Both these initiatives were intended to redress what supporters saw as a government bias against religious programs, making it easier for the government to support social services that were affiliated with religious groups or philosophies.

But both initiatives were hobbled by the suspicion that they would not pass muster with the Supreme Court because they violated the First Amendment. Now, with the voucher decision, the shadow of unconstitutionality has been lifted, according to a wide range of experts on church-state issues.

"The one thing that's clear out of this decision is that the faith-based initiative is affirmed, it is approved, it is not a constitutional problem," said Jay Sekulow, chief counsel of the American Center for Law and Justice, a conservative law firm that filed a friend-of-the-court brief supporting the Cleveland voucher plan.

Even those who have reservations about vouchers say they believe the ruling will be more broadly applied. "Any kind of voucher arrangements for government grants to religious groups for social services are now certainly going to be seen as not only possible, but constitutional," said Charles C. Haynes, senior scholar at the Freedom Forum First Amendment Center in Arlington, Va.

"More broadly," Mr. Haynes added, "I think this ruling signals that the court does not any longer worry too much that government money may eventually end up with religious institutions. And that is a major change. It may mark a turning point in how the government relates to religion in the United States."

The strict wall of separation between church and state gradually erected through a series of court rulings in the 1970's and 1980's is now gradually being dismantled, the experts said. Recent rulings have held that religion is entitled to equal treatment in public life. For instance, a Supreme Court decision last year found that if the Boy Scouts and the 4-H Club can meet at a public school, so can a Bible study class.

The decision Wednesday by the United States Court of Appeals for the Ninth Circuit that the phrase "one nation under God" in the Pledge of Allegiance is unconstitutional is likely to be seen in the long run as an aberration for this era, many experts said.

"I never make predictions, but I predict that decision will be reversed," Mr. Hasson said of the appeals court ruling. "When it is simply a generic reference to God it can no more be interpreted as official religion than reading the Declaration of Independence, which says that all men are endowed by their creator with certain unalienable rights."

Many people say the effects of the Cleveland decision will soon be felt. Religious groups may meet less resistance to using government tax-free bonds to finance construction of hospitals or universities, Mr. Sekulow suggested. So might students who have been barred in some states from using government scholarships in religious colleges or seminaries.

However, legislators who read the decision closely will find there are limitations, said Marc Stern, legal director for the American Jewish Congress, which supported the plaintiff in the Cleveland case.

The Ohio statute said that the vouchers could not be used at religious schools that discriminated on the basis of religion, or that taught the superiority of any religion or religious hatred, Mr. Stern said.

The Supreme Court's decision was also premised on the idea that parents would have "genuine choice" — that they would be able to use their vouchers at an array of religious and nonreligious schools. But many states and localities that will now move to activate vouchers for schools and social service programs are not likely to be able to offer a range of religious and secular choices.

Nevertheless, Mr. Stern, too, predicted that this would not put a damper on enthusiasm for the voucher approach.

"We are going to see a wave of legislation trying to funnel government money to religious schools and programs," he said. "All the caveats are going to be ignored because people don't read opinions. They're just going to see this as a green light."

Judge's Biblical Monument Is Ruled Unconstitutional

BY JEFFREY GETTLEMAN | NOV. 19, 2002

MONTGOMERY, ALA., NOV. 18 — Roy Moore may be the chief justice of the Alabama Supreme Court, but around here most people just call him the Ten Commandments judge.

And the 5,280-pound monument of the holy tablets he wheeled into his courthouse early one morning last year, without the knowledge of his colleagues, is simply known as "Roy's rock."

Almost instantly the chunk of granite became a beacon, a shining light across the South, drawing fundamentalist Christians to Montgomery by the busload. Many dropped to their knees in front of the monument and prayed.

Civil liberties groups accused Justice Moore of turning a courthouse into a church. But his popularity only grew. Not long ago, Justice Moore was a little-known county judge with a homemade plaque of the Ten Commandments tacked to his courtroom wall. Now he was an Alabama folk hero.

But today a federal judge issued his own commandment: Thou shalt remove thy monument. Now.

"This court holds that the evidence is overwhelming and the law is clear that the chief justice violated the Establishment Clause," wrote Judge Myron H. Thompson of Federal District Court in Montgomery in a crackling opinion, referring to a clause in the First Amendment. The monument is "nothing less than an obtrusive year-round religious display intended to proselytize on behalf of a particular religion, the chief justice's religion."

In Alabama, there is no underestimating the popularity of religion — and defiance. While fundamentalists in Kansas lost their battle for creationism, and supporters of organized school prayer were defeated in Texas, evangelical Christians still set the agenda here. This is the state, after all, where high school science books have stickers on them saying evolution is just a theory.

Justice Moore tapped right into this, becoming a figurehead in the movement pushing for more religion in public life. The 55-year-old judge, a former ranch hand and kickboxer, does radio shows, helps raise money for evangelical groups and travels roads near and far in his old blue Cadillac, promoting his unique blend of church and state.

Today's decision was hailed by civil liberties groups as proof that there are limits.

"Justice Moore was elected to administer justice, not to serve as a religious minister," said Richard Cohen, general counsel of the Southern Poverty Law Center, one of the parties that sued last month to have the Ten Commandments removed.

Justice Moore's lawyer said the federal courts were "confused." He vowed to appeal today's ruling.

Justice Moore had repeatedly said he would never remove the monument, a four-foot-high cube that rises from the lobby floor. It was one of his campaign pledges two years ago to bring the Ten Commandments to the State Supreme Court.

He has also rejected requests from outside groups to display other monuments in the courthouse. By state law, it is his decision. In the chief justice's pocket are the courthouse keys. An alliance of black organizations asked to put up a plaque of the Rev. Dr. Martin Luther King Jr.'s "I Have a Dream" speech. Justice Moore said no. Ditto for the atheist group that wanted to display a statue of an atom.

The roots of the case go back to 1992, when Justice Moore was appointed as a judge in Etowah County, in northwestern Alabama. One of his first acts was to hang a homemade rosewood plaque of the Ten Commandments in his courtroom.

Three years later, the A.C.L.U. sued. The first judge ordered Judge Moore to take it down. Judge Moore refused. Then Gov. Fob James Jr. vowed to send in the National Guard to protect Judge Moore's plaque.

The Ten Commandments monument at the State Supreme Court draws fundamentalist Christians to Montgomery, Ala., by the busload. Many have dropped to their knees in front of it and prayed.

Judge Moore became a cause célèbre, sending his name recognition into a realm that few other judges this side of Lance Ito ever enjoy.

He emerged a contender for chief justice of the State Supreme Court and won easily in November 2000.

The next August, early one morning, he sneaked the cube monument, paid for by an evangelical group, into the court building. He did not tell any of the eight other justices.

A Montgomery lawyer, Stephen R. Glassroth, who is Jewish, then sued.

"It offends me going to work everyday and coming face to face with that symbol, which says to me that the state endorses Judge Moore's version of the Judeo-Christian God above all others," Mr. Glassroth said.

Last month, a weeklong trial was held in federal court. Presiding was Judge Thompson, an appointee of President Jimmy Carter.

Justice Moore argued that the monument did not establish a state religion but merely acknowledged the role God had played throughout the history of American law.

"I feel very strongly that the monument represents the moral foundation of law, which is greatly needed in our country today," he said.

After mulling over his decision for a month, Judge Thompson issued a 93-page opinion today, saying Justice Moore had violated the separation between church and state.

"The only way to miss the religious or nonsecular appearance of the monument would be to walk through the Alabama State Judicial Building with one's eyes closed," he wrote.

Judge Thompson said the display was much different from other displays of the Ten Commandments, including one at the United States Supreme Court, which is incorporated with other symbols.

He gave Justice Moore 30 days to get the monument out of the courthouse.

Christian groups in Alabama said they were not giving up.

"We anticipate wide-ranging resistance to the removal of this monument," the president of the Christian Coalition of Alabama, John Giles, said.

Danielle J. Lipow, who delivered the closing argument for the Southern Poverty Law Center, said that the case against Justice Moore and his monument was not an attack on anyone who holds strong religious beliefs.

"Judge Moore has every right to believe what he does about the role of God and the state," Ms. Lipow said. "What this case does is establish that Judge Moore does not have the right to impose that view on others through state policy. That's the danger."

In Order, President Eases Limits on U.S. Aid to Religious Groups

BY RICHARD W. STEVENSON | DEC. 13, 2002

PRESIDENT BUSH ACTED today to make it easier for religious organizations to receive federal money for social welfare programs, invoking both executive powers and his belief in the power of faith to help society's neediest people.

His move on one of his signature issues was applauded by religious and community organizations and by many conservatives as a way to encourage churches, synagogues, mosques and groups associated with them to do more to help the poor, the sick and the troubled. But it was criticized by some Democrats and civil liberties groups as an infringement on the separation of church and state and a step backward on discrimination in hiring.

People on both sides of the issue said the most important element of Mr. Bush's action was its assertion that federal law does not require religious groups to give up their right to hire on the basis of religious belief just because they become federal contractors. A dispute over how to deal with hiring discrimination was the main reason Mr. Bush's proposals in support of religion-based charitable work — a centerpiece of his presidential campaign and one of the first pieces of legislation he sought from Congress after taking office — have languished in the Senate.

Mr. Bush, whose action today was an effort to break that logjam, said he wanted to continue pursuing legislation on the issue. But he took the action despite the shift in control in the Senate to Republican from Democratic, leading some of his critics to say he had gone farther through his own powers than even his own party would be willing to go legislatively.

In an executive order, Mr. Bush broadly required that federal agencies not discriminate against religious organizations in awarding money to community and social services groups for programs to help people in need.

Mr. Bush also signed a separate executive order establishing offices of religion-based initiatives in the Agriculture Department and the Agency for International Development, joining similar offices already established in five other big government agencies. And he directed the Federal Emergency Management Agency to allow religious nonprofit groups to qualify for aid after disasters like earthquakes and hurricanes in the same way that secular nonprofit groups can qualify.

The president's speech here announcing the actions was infused with references to faith and was built around the idea that religion can and should occupy a central place in both public and private life.

"Through all these actions, I hope that every faith-based group in America, the social entrepreneurs of America, understand that this government respects your work and we respect the motivation behind your work," Mr. Bush said. "We do not want you to become carbon copies of public programs. We want you to follow your heart. We want you to follow the word. We want you to do the works of kindness and mercy you are called upon to do."

Speaking in forceful and often emotional terms that drew repeated "amens" and applause from a lunchtime crowd of people involved in religion-based community programs, Mr. Bush drew a distinction between government financing for religious activities, which he said was wrong, and government financing for efforts by groups with religious ties to help the neediest.

"If a charity is helping the needy, it should not matter if there is a rabbi on the board, or a cross or a crescent on the wall, or a religious commitment in the charter," he said. "The days of discriminating against religious groups just because they are religious are coming to an end."

But Democrats said Mr. Bush's action undermined a legal principle dating to 1941 under which groups that receive federal financing must adhere to nondiscrimination standards. They said it would do so by allowing religious organizations not only to hire only people of their own faith, but also potentially to rule out some job seekers on the basis of other factors like sexual orientation that might clash with their religion's tenets.

"Under the new rule, organizations can accept public funds and then refuse to employ persons because they are Jewish, Catholic, unmarried, gay or lesbian," said Senator Edward M. Kennedy, Democrat of Massachusetts. "Rather than use the faith-based initiative to undermine our national commitment to civil rights, the president's executive order should have made clear that no organization receiving taxpayer money can discriminate in its services or its employment practices."

Christopher Anders, legislative counsel for the American Civil Liberties Union in Washington, said Mr. Bush had "accomplished at the stroke of a pen what he couldn't get through Congress in the last two years and what he calculated he couldn't even get from a Republican Congress next year, which is a tremendous rollback to civil rights protections."

James Towey, the director of the White House's Office of Faith-Based Initiatives, said Mr. Bush's action was consistent with federal law holding that religious groups are permitted to hire on the basis of religion. He said it would apply to groups that receive federal contracts of $10,000 or more, but not federal grants.

"The president simply feels that this executive order will clarify that these groups keep that civil right they have when they do federal contracting," Mr. Towey told reporters this morning on Air Force One.

Asked whether Mr. Bush believed that religious groups would be able to discriminate based on characteristics like sexual orientation, a senior administration official said the president believes religion-based organizations "should be able to hire people that support their vision and mission" in a way consistent with previous court rulings on the issue.

The president's effort to promote religion-based social programs has met with a mixed reaction from religious groups. It has been opposed by most mainline Protestants, such as the president's own denomination, the United Methodist Church, and by most Reform and Conservative Jewish groups. It has been supported by most evangelical and Orthodox Jewish groups, while African American denominations have been split.

Mr. Bush's efforts to promote his religion-based agenda have taken on extra political resonance in recent weeks. Esquire magazine recently published a story quoting John DiIulio, the first head of the White House's religion-based office, saying politics had trumped policy making within the administration. Mr. DiIulio — who is from Philadelphia, where Mr. Bush spoke today — later apologized and said his statements had been baseless. But Democrats have seized on them to suggest that Mr. Bush is driven by a desire to please his party's right wing.

The president's move today took by surprise some groups that had been monitoring Mr. Bush's efforts. On Monday, leaders of the National Association for the Advancement of Colored People, the Leadership Committee on Civil Rights, the American Association of University Women and Americans United for Separation of Church and State met with Mr. Towey. Some of the people present at the meeting said Mr. Towey gave no indication that the president was about to take the action he took today.

Representatives of some of those groups said today that they were outraged.

But Mr. Bush won cautious support from Senator Joseph I. Lieberman, Democrat of Connecticut. He said that Mr. Bush's executive order did not appear to usurp existing state and local civil rights laws and that "on the surface it sounds like a sound plan for realizing the principle of equal treatment for faith-based groups."

Boston Archdiocese Asks for Dismissal of All Suits

BY ADAM LIPTAK | DEC. 24, 2002

THE ROMAN CATHOLIC Archdiocese of Boston asked a judge yesterday to dismiss all the sexual abuse lawsuits against it on religious freedom grounds.

The First Amendment, the archdiocese said, does not permit courts to tell churches how to conduct their internal affairs, including the questions of where to assign priests and how to discipline them.

Bishop Richard G. Lennon, the archdiocese's interim leader, said the motion to dismiss the suits, which number more than 400, did not indicate a change in his commitment to trying to settle them. Rather, he said, the move was driven by the archdiocese's insurers and by a motion-filing deadline set by Judge Constance M. Sweeney of Suffolk Superior Court, who is hearing the cases.

Bishop Lennon also renewed his request that lawyers for the plaintiffs agree to a moratorium on further court proceedings and on the exchange of information between the parties. That, he said in proposing such a moratorium last week, would enable the two sides to concentrate on reaching a settlement.

Legal experts said that the First Amendment approach had little chance of success but that the archdiocese might well have jeopardized its insurance coverage had it failed to pursue any available arguments.

Jeffrey A. Newman, a lawyer for plaintiffs who say they were victims of the Rev. Paul R. Shanley, expressed appreciation for the explanation of the filing, and largely accepted the archdiocese's reasoning.

"The concern existed on the part of the archdiocese," Mr. Newman said, "that filing the motion would inflame an almost dangerously incendiary atmosphere by suggesting it was not serious in trying to resolve these claims."

But Mr. Newman was unimpressed by the argument that the First Amendment bars suits based on accusations of sexual abuse and cover-ups. "They don't make sense," he said of the First Amendment defenses, "to the extent you're talking about actions as opposed to beliefs."

Mitchell Garabedian, who represents other plaintiffs, concurred. "Child molestation qualifies as conduct that disturbs the public order and thus is not entitled to constitutional protection," he said.

Nor was either lawyer inclined to agree to a litigation moratorium, though Mr. Newman said that if the archdiocese's insurers were to make a significant offer, the pace of the litigation might slow.

Legal experts said First Amendment defenses like those in the new motion had met with some success in earlier cases. But the defenses have little hope, they said, in the current charged atmosphere.

"All of these claims do have a First Amendment implication about how churches select, train and supervise clergy," said Douglas J. Laycock, a law professor at the University of Texas who is an expert in the law of religious liberty. "The churches have won a few, but they have lost a lot more. It's not that they are clearly wrong arguments, but they have had declining success over the years. And the courts may not be immune to the incredible publicity of the last year, either."

Arguments about religious freedom, he said, are more likely to be accepted when the asserted abuses were isolated and supervisors acted on limited information.

A number of courts around the country have held the church immune from suit for the negligent hiring and supervision of priests who engage in sexual abuse. In 1997, for instance, the Wisconsin Supreme Court rejected a claim that the church had negligently supervised a hospital chaplain who was accused of sexually assaulting a woman. The court said it could not decide the case without interpreting ecclesiastical law, particularly the vow of celibacy. That, it held, would "excessively entangle the court in religious affairs, contrary to the First Amendment."

The majority of courts, though, have taken the opposite view. In March, the Florida Supreme Court held that "the First Amendment does not provide a shield behind which a church" may hide when accusations of sexual abuse are made.

In Massachusetts, the courts have tried to distinguish between matters of doctrine and harmful conduct. "The First Amendment prohibits civil courts from intervening in disputes concerning religious doctrine, discipline, faith or internal organization," the state's highest court held in 1985. In various cases since, courts have sidestepped disputes about hiring and firing clergymen and how churches govern themselves.

But they have not hesitated to decide suits concerning discrimination by churches acting as landlords and about the use of drugs in religious ceremonies. And they have shown special solicitude for claims concerning the health and safety of children.

In 1999, in a decision in a case against John J. Geoghan, the former priest whose case ignited the sexual abuse crisis, Judge James F. McHugh rejected most of the First Amendment arguments made anew yesterday. "The delicate balance between the freedom to exercise religion and the demands placed on all persons, clergy and others, to refrain from conduct with harmful potential to others," Judge McHugh wrote, "requires the courts to avoid sweeping, categorical decisions."

But he denied the motion, and legal experts say there is little reason to think other judges will do otherwise.

The White House Puts the Bible Before the Hippocratic Oath

EDITORIAL | BY THE NEW YORK TIMES | JAN. 28, 2018

TAMESHA MEANS HAD been pregnant for just 18 weeks when her water broke in 2010. In pain, she rushed to a hospital near her house in Michigan. But because it was a Catholic health center, doctors there did not tell her that continuing her pregnancy could threaten her health and that abortion was her safest option. Instead they sent her home. They did so again when she returned the next day, bleeding, with painful contractions. They were preparing to send her home for a third time when she miscarried at the hospital.

Cases like this, in which a provider's religious beliefs take precedence over a patient's needs, could become more common because of a series of recent White House decisions that please the anti-abortion movement. The decisions may make it more difficult for teenagers wanting to get tested for sexually transmitted diseases, for gay men looking to prevent HIV and even for women seeking breast exams or pap smears.

Earlier this month, the Department of Health and Human Services announced the creation of a "Conscience and Religious Freedom Division" to enforce laws protecting health care providers' right to opt out of certain procedures, including post-abortion care or gender-affirming surgery, because of religious objections. (The website displays what appears to be a female Muslim doctor in a hijab smiling enthusiastically — a twist on the administration's usual attitude toward Muslims.)

The unveiling of the new office may simply be a signal to the conservative base, an elaborate way of saying, "We haven't been able to ban abortions after the 20th week of pregnancy, but we still care."

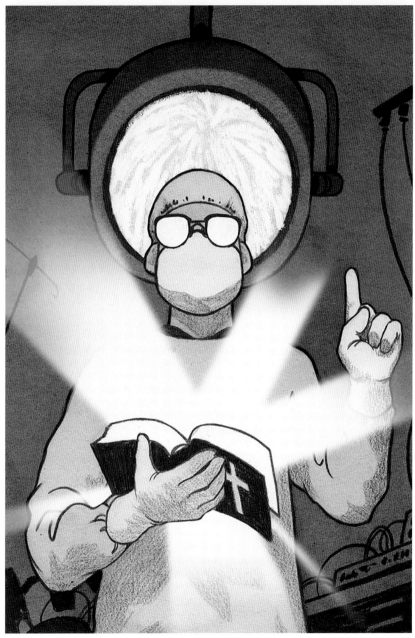

LEONARDO SANTAMARIA

But the administration also released a 216-page proposed rule detailing how the new division will double down on religious protections. Right now, state and federal laws already protect a nurse, for instance, who doesn't want to assist with an abortion for religious reasons. But in a list of definitions, the administration would expand the meaning of "assisting" to include making referrals to a different provider, or even simply counseling a patient on her options. In the same list, the department broadly redefines "work force" so religious protections can apply not just to the nurse in the room, but also to the scheduler, the janitor and the security guard outside.

"The definition of 'to assist' is unparalleled," said Louise Melling, the deputy legal director of the American Civil Liberties Union. "It goes so far as to include someone objecting to checking you in, someone objecting to doing your insurance paperwork, someone objecting to even taking your temperature."

The regulations don't recommend that doctors balance a patient's needs with religious objections; religious objections are given top priority.

The rule suggests that the office can investigate a health care entity not just based on actual complaints, but also based on "threatened" or "potential" ones.

There could also be grim consequences from a one-page letter the administration sent to state Medicaid directors, suggesting that they may now block Medicaid funding for Planned Parenthood or other health centers that provide abortions. (Planned Parenthood says that more than half of its patients are covered by Medicaid.) The letter overturned a 2016 Obama-era directive that required states to distribute federal funds for family planning services, like contraception, prenatal care and testing for sexually transmitted diseases, to qualified health providers, regardless of whether those providers also perform abortions.

Freedom of religion is essential — and so is access to health care. Current law tries to accommodate both, but the far right has stirred unfounded fears that religion (and Christianity in particular) is under assault, and that people of faith are in danger of being forced to do things they find morally objectionable. "Patient-centered care" is an important goal in clinical training today, but the administration is instead proposing provider-centered care.

In recent conflicts between patient needs and religious freedom, patients have too often lost. The Trump administration wants to keep it that way.

What Islamophobic Politicians Can Learn From Mormons

OPINION | BY ASMA UDDIN | MAY 22, 2018

LAST MONTH, THE Supreme Court heard oral arguments on President Trump's travel ban, popularly known as the "Muslim ban" because of his statements, like one in 2015 calling for "a total and complete shutdown of Muslims entering the United States."

But Mr. Trump is far from the only Republican willing to discriminate against Muslims. BuzzFeed News reported in April that since 2015, Republican officials in 49 states have publicly attacked Islam, some even questioning its legitimacy as a religion.

The only exception? Utah. In that state, where a majority of residents is Mormon, members of the Church of Jesus Christ of Latter-day Saints, elected officials seem to have a deep understanding that an attack on the religious freedom of one group is an attack on the religious freedom of everyone. The rest of the nation should follow their example.

Utah's politicians stand out against many of those whose statements BuzzFeed News chronicled, like an Oklahoma state representative named John Bennett, who in 2014 called Islam "a cancer," and last year met with Muslim constituents only after they filled out questionnaires asking whether they beat their wives. A Nebraska state senator, Bill Kintner, proposed that Muslims be required to eat pork if they wished to enter the United States. A state senator in Rhode Island, Elaine Morgan, wrote that "Muslim religion and philosophy is to murder, rape and decapitate anyone who is a non-Muslim" and recommended that Syrian refugees be housed in camps. She later said she was referring only to "fanatical/extremist" Muslims.

In January, Neal Tapio, a South Dakota state senator who is running for the United States House, questioned whether the First Amendment applies to Muslims, asking, "Does our Constitution offer protections and rights to a person who believes in the full implementation of Islamic law, as practiced by 14 Islamic countries" and millions of Muslims "who believe in the deadly political ideology that believes you should be killed for leaving Islam?"

Representative Bennett, the lawmaker who required Muslim constituents to answer questionnaires on whether they beat their wives, said in 2014, "Islam is not even a religion; it is a social, political system that uses a deity to advance its agenda of global conquest."

Jody Hice, a 2014 Republican congressional candidate from Georgia, questioned the compatibility of Islam with the American Constitution and wrote in 2012 that "Islam would not qualify for First Amendment protection since it's a geopolitical system."

And yet, in Utah — one of the most crimson-red states in the Union — such rhetoric is conspicuously absent.

"I'd be the first to stand up for their rights," said Utah's senior senator, Orrin Hatch, in 2010 amid the controversy surrounding the construction of an Islamic community center close to ground zero in New York City. He called Islam "a great religion."

Utah's other Republican senator, Mike Lee, said he did not vote for Donald Trump in part because he saw the travel ban as a "religious test." In explaining why many in Utah opposed the ban, Utah's Republican governor, Gary Herbert, observed, "We had Rutherford B. Hayes in 1879 issue an envoy to Europe saying in essence, 'Don't send those Mormon immigrants to America anymore.' "

Pointing to this history of Mormon persecution, in 2017, a group of scholars with expertise in Mormon history filed an amicus brief in the United States Court of Appeals for the Ninth Circuit opposing the ban. They drew a comparison between the government's current posture toward Muslims and the government's 19th-century treatment of Mormons. "This court should ensure that history does not repeat itself," they wrote.

Mormon politicians seem to understand better than many of their fellow Republicans that if another's freedom of faith is under attack, so, too, is their own. Perhaps this has to do with the church's 11th Article of Faith, which states, "We claim the privilege of worshiping Almighty God according to the dictates of our own conscience, and allow all men the same privilege, let them worship how, where or what they may."

Their interest in the rights of people of other faiths has also been traced to the views of the Mormon founder Joseph Smith, who put it this way: "If it has been demonstrated that I have been willing to die for a Mormon, I am bold to declare before Heaven that I am just as ready to die in defending the rights of a Presbyterian, a Baptist or a good man of any denomination."

Mormons know too well what it means to be singled out for persecution, and to have one's faith maligned as a threat to America. But it shouldn't require that experience to understand that religious freedom for some is really religious freedom for none.

ASMA T. UDDIN, a religious liberty lawyer and scholar, is working on a book about American Muslims and the First Amendment.

In Narrow Decision, Supreme Court Sides With Baker Who Turned Away Gay Couple

BY ADAM LIPTAK | JUNE 4, 2018

WASHINGTON — The Supreme Court on Monday ruled in favor of a Colorado baker who had refused to create a wedding cake for a gay couple. The court's decision was narrow, and it left open the larger question of whether a business can discriminate against gay men and lesbians based on rights protected by the First Amendment.

The court passed on an opportunity to either bolster the right to same-sex marriage or explain how far the government can go in regulating businesses run on religious principles. Instead, Justice Anthony M. Kennedy's majority opinion turned on the argument that the Colorado Civil Rights Commission, which originally ruled against the baker, had been shown to be hostile to religion because of the remarks of one of its members.

At the same time, Justice Kennedy strongly reaffirmed protections for gay rights.

"The outcome of cases like this in other circumstances must await further elaboration in the courts," he wrote, "all in the context of recognizing that these disputes must be resolved with tolerance, without undue disrespect to sincere religious beliefs, and without subjecting gay persons to indignities when they seek goods and services in an open market."

Justice Kennedy often casts the deciding vote in closely divided cases on major social issues. When the court agreed to hear the Colorado case last June, it seemed to present him with a stark choice between two of his core commitments. On the one hand, Justice Kennedy has written every major Supreme Court decision protecting gay men and lesbians. On the other, he is the court's most ardent defender of free speech.

On Monday, Justice Kennedy chose a third path, one that seemed to apply only to the case before the court.

Writing for the majority in the 7 to-2 decision, he said the Civil Rights Commission's ruling against the baker, Jack Phillips, had been infected by religious animus. He cited what he said were "inappropriate and dismissive comments" from one commissioner in saying that the panel had acted inappropriately and that its decision should be overturned.

"The neutral and respectful consideration to which Phillips was entitled was compromised here," Justice Kennedy wrote. "The Civil Rights Commission's treatment of his case has some elements of a clear and impermissible hostility toward the sincere religious beliefs that motivated his objection."

That passage echoed his plea for tolerance in his majority opinion in 2015 in Obergefell v. Hodges, which recognized a constitutional right to same-sex marriage. In that decision, he called for "an open and searching debate" between those who opposed same-sex marriage on religious grounds and those who considered such unions "proper or indeed essential."

When the Colorado case was argued in December, Justice Kennedy seemed frustrated with the main choices available to him and hinted that he was looking for an off ramp. His questions suggested that his vote had not been among the four that had been needed to add the case to the court's docket.

The breadth of the court's majority was a testament to the narrowness of the decision's reasoning. Chief Justice John G. Roberts Jr. and Justices Stephen G. Breyer, Samuel A. Alito Jr., Elena Kagan and Neil M. Gorsuch joined Justice Kennedy's majority opinion. Justice Clarence Thomas voted with the majority but would have adopted broader reasons.

Justice Ruth Bader Ginsburg, joined by Justice Sonia Sotomayor, dissented.

The case, Masterpiece Cakeshop v. Colorado Civil Rights Commission, No. 16-111, arose from a brief encounter in 2012, when David

Jack Phillips, the owner of Masterpiece Cakeshop, leaving the Supreme Court in December. The court said on Monday that a Colorado panel's decision against him had been infected by religious animus.

Mullins and Charlie Craig visited Mr. Phillips's bakery, Masterpiece Cakeshop, in Lakewood, Colo. The two men were going to be married in Massachusetts, and they were looking for a wedding cake for a reception in Colorado.

Mr. Phillips turned them down, saying he would not use his talents to convey a message of support for same-sex marriage at odds with his religious faith. Mr. Mullins and Mr. Craig said they were humiliated by Mr. Phillips's refusal to serve them, and they filed a complaint with Colorado's Civil Rights Commission, saying that Mr. Phillips had violated a state law barring discrimination based on sexual orientation.

Mr. Mullins and Mr. Craig won before the commission and in the state courts.

The Colorado Court of Appeals ruled that Mr. Phillips's free speech rights had not been violated, noting that the couple had not discussed the cake's design before Mr. Phillips turned them down. The court added that people seeing the cake would not understand Mr. Phillips to be making a statement and that he remained free to say what he liked about same sex marriage in other settings.

Though the case was mostly litigated on free speech grounds, Justice Kennedy's opinion barely discussed the issue. Instead, he focused on what he said were flaws in the proceedings before the commission. Members of the panel, he wrote, had acted with "clear and impermissible hostility" to sincerely held religious beliefs.

One commissioner in particular, Justice Kennedy wrote, had crossed the line in saying that "freedom of religion and religion has been used to justify all kinds of discrimination throughout history, whether it be slavery, whether it be the Holocaust."

Justice Kennedy wrote that "this sentiment is inappropriate for a commission charged with the solemn responsibility of fair and neutral enforcement of Colorado's anti-discrimination law."

In dissent, Justice Ginsburg said that a few stray remarks were not enough to justify a ruling in Mr. Phillips's favor.

"What prejudice infected the determinations of the adjudicators in the case before and after the commission?" Justice Ginsburg asked. "The court does not say."

Justice Kennedy wrote that the commission had also acted inconsistently in cases involving an opponent of same-sex marriage, "concluding on at least three occasions that a baker acted lawfully in declining to create cakes with decorations that demeaned gay persons or gay marriages."

In dueling concurring opinions, two sets of justices debated how central that last observation was to the court's decision. Justice Kagan, joined by Justice Breyer, said such differing treatment could be justified. Justice Gorsuch, joined by Justice Alito, disagreed, saying that "the two cases share all legally salient features."

In another concurring opinion, Justice Thomas, joined by Justice Gorsuch, said he would have ruled in favor of Mr. Phillips on free speech grounds. Mr. Phillips's cakes are artistic expression worthy of First Amendment protection, Justice Thomas wrote, and requiring him to endorse marriages at odds with his faith violated his constitutional rights.

In dissent, Justice Ginsburg disagreed with that analysis and noted that the majority had not adopted it. She wrote that there was reason to think that people seeing a wedding cake made by Mr. Phillips would understand it to be conveying his views on same-sex marriage.

Alliance Defending Freedom, which represented Mr. Phillips, said the ruling was a victory for religious liberty.

"Government hostility toward people of faith has no place in our society, yet the State of Colorado was openly antagonistic toward Jack's religious beliefs about marriage," said Kristen Waggoner, a lawyer with the group. "The court was right to condemn that. Tolerance and respect for good-faith differences of opinion are essential in a society like ours."

TOM BRENNER/THE NEW YORK TIMES

Protesters outside the Supreme Court after the ruling, which one gay rights group said "offered dangerous encouragement to those who would deny civil rights to L.G.B.T. people."

The American Civil Liberties Union, which represented Mr. Mullins and Mr. Craig, said it welcomed the parts of the majority opinion that reaffirmed legal protections for gay men and lesbians.

"The court reversed the Masterpiece Cakeshop decision based on concerns unique to the case but reaffirmed its longstanding rule that states can prevent the harms of discrimination in the marketplace, including against L.G.B.T. people," said Louise Melling, the group's deputy legal director.

Some gay rights groups took a darker view of the decision. "The court today has offered dangerous encouragement to those who would deny civil rights to L.G.B.T. people," said Rachel B. Tiven, the chief executive of Lambda Legal. "We will fiercely resist the coming effort that will seek to turn this ruling into a broad license to discriminate."

Even as she dissented, Justice Ginsburg wrote that "there is much in the court's opinion with which I agree," quoting several passages reaffirming gay rights protections.

"Colorado law," Justice Kennedy wrote in one, "can protect gay persons, just as it can protect other classes of individuals, in acquiring whatever products and services they choose on the same terms and conditions as are offered to other members of the public."

Trump's Travel Ban Is Upheld by Supreme Court

BY ADAM LIPTAK AND MICHAEL D. SHEAR | JUNE 26, 2018

WASHINGTON — The Supreme Court upheld President Trump's ban on travel from several predominantly Muslim countries, delivering to the president on Tuesday a political victory and an endorsement of his power to control immigration at a time of political upheaval about the treatment of migrants at the Mexican border.

In a 5-to-4 vote, the court's conservatives said that the president's power to secure the country's borders, delegated by Congress over decades of immigration lawmaking, was not undermined by Mr. Trump's history of incendiary statements about the dangers he said Muslims pose to the United States.

Writing for the majority, Chief Justice John G. Roberts Jr. said that Mr. Trump had ample statutory authority to make national security judgments in the realm of immigration. And the chief justice rejected a constitutional challenge to Mr. Trump's third executive order on the matter, issued in September as a proclamation.

The court's liberals denounced the decision. In a passionate and searing dissent from the bench, Justice Sonia Sotomayor said the decision was no better than Korematsu v. United States, the 1944 decision that endorsed the detention of Japanese-Americans during World War II.

She praised the court for officially overturning Korematsu in its decision on Tuesday. But by upholding the travel ban, Justice Sotomayor said, the court "merely replaces one gravely wrong decision with another."

The court's travel ban decision provides new political ammunition for the president and members of his party as they prepare to face the voters in the fall. Mr. Trump has already made clear his plans to use anti-immigrant messaging as he campaigns for Republicans, much the way he successfully deployed the issue to whip up the base of the party during the 2016 presidential campaign.

Mr. Trump, who has battled court challenges to the travel ban since the first days of his administration, hailed the decision to uphold his third version as a "tremendous victory" and promised to continue using his office to defend the country against terrorism, crime and extremism.

"This ruling is also a moment of profound vindication following months of hysterical commentary from the media and Democratic politicians who refuse to do what it takes to secure our border and our country," the president said in a statement issued by the White House soon after the decision was announced.

The vindication for Mr. Trump was also a stunning political validation of the Republican strategy of obstruction throughout 2016 that prevented President Barack Obama from seating Judge Merrick B. Garland on the nation's highest court after the death of Justice Antonin Scalia. Justice Neil M. Gorsuch, Mr. Trump's choice to sit on the court, was part of the majority upholding the president's travel ban.

The decision came even as Mr. Trump is facing controversy over his decision to impose "zero tolerance" for illegal immigration at the United States' southwestern border, leading to politically damaging images of children being separated from their parents as families cross into the country without proper documentation.

But as Mr. Trump celebrated his travel ban victory, a federal judge in California ordered the government to stop separating children from their parents at the border and to reunite families already separated.

Late Tuesday night, the judge said that all families must be reunited within 30 days and that children under 5 must be returned to the custody of their parents within two weeks.

The judge's order came as the president faces a second legal challenge about the family separations. Seventeen states and the District of Columbia filed a lawsuit on Tuesday in federal court seeking to stop the practice.

Mr. Trump and his advisers have long argued that presidents are given vast authority to reshape the way that the United States controls its borders. The president's attempts to do that began with the travel ban and continues today with his demand for an end to the "catch and release" of unauthorized immigrants.

In remarks on Tuesday in a meeting with lawmakers, Mr. Trump vowed to continue fighting for a wall across the southern border with Mexico — his favorite physical manifestation of the legal powers that the court says he rightly wields.

"We have to be tough and we have to be safe and we have to be secure," he said, adding that construction of the wall "stops the drugs."

"It stops people we don't want to have," the president said.

Several hundred angry protesters gathered in Washington on the court's marble steps with signs that read, "No Ban, No Wall," "Resist Trump's Hate" and "Refugees Welcome!"

In New York City, about three dozen activists, government officials and concerned citizens declared at a midday news conference that the court was on the "wrong side of history." Bitta Mostofi, the commissioner of immigrant affairs for the New York mayor's office, called the ruling an "institutionalization of Islamophobia and racism."

Senator Robert Menendez, Democrat of New Jersey, wrote that "today is a sad day for American institutions, and for all religious minorities who have ever sought refuge in a land promising freedom." The Baptist Joint Committee for Religious Liberty said in a statement that "we are deeply disappointed by the Supreme Court's refusal to repudiate policy rooted in animus against Muslims."

Mr. Trump's ban on travel had been in place since December, when the court denied a request from challengers to block it. Tuesday's ruling lifts the legal cloud over the policy.

Chief Justice Roberts acknowledged that Mr. Trump had made many statements concerning his desire to impose a "Muslim ban." He recounted the president's call for a "total and complete shutdown of Muslims entering the United States," and he noted that the president has said that "Islam hates us" and has asserted that the United States was "having problems with Muslims coming into the country."

But the chief justice said the president's comments must be balanced against the powers of the president to conduct the national security affairs of the nation.

"The issue before us is not whether to denounce the statements," Chief Justice Roberts wrote. "It is instead the significance of those statements in reviewing a presidential directive, neutral on its face, addressing a matter within the core of executive responsibility."

"In doing so," he wrote, "we must consider not only the statements of a particular president, but also the authority of the presidency itself."

The chief justice repeatedly echoed Stephen Miller, Mr. Trump's top immigration adviser, in citing a provision of immigration law that gives presidents the power to "suspend the entry of all aliens or any class of aliens" as they see necessary.

The provision "exudes deference to the president in every clause," the chief justice said.

He concluded that Mr. Trump's proclamation, viewed in isolation, was neutral and justified by national security concerns. Chief Justice Roberts wrote it is "expressly premised on legitimate purposes: preventing entry of nationals who cannot be adequately vetted and inducing other nations to improve their practices."

Even as it upheld the travel ban, the court's majority took a momentous step. It overruled the Korematsu case, officially reversing a wartime ruling that for decades has stood as an emblem of a morally repugnant response to fear.

Chief Justice Roberts said Tuesday's decision was very different.

"The forcible relocation of U.S. citizens to concentration camps, solely and explicitly on the basis of race, is objectively unlawful and outside the scope of presidential authority," he wrote. "But it is wholly inapt to liken that morally repugnant order to a facially neutral policy denying certain foreign nationals the privilege of admission."

"The entry suspension is an act that is well within executive authority and could have been taken by any other president — the only question is evaluating the actions of this particular president in promulgating an otherwise valid proclamation," Chief Justice Roberts wrote.

Justices Anthony M. Kennedy, Clarence Thomas, Samuel A. Alito Jr. also joined the majority opinion.

In her dissent, Justice Sotomayor lashed out at Mr. Trump, also quoting many of the anti-Muslim statements. She noted that, on Twitter, he retweeted three anti-Muslim videos as president and tweeted that "we need a TRAVEL BAN for certain DANGEROUS countries."

"Let the gravity of those statements sink in," Justice Sotomayor said. "Most of these words were spoken or written by the current president of the United States."

She dismissed the majority's conclusion that the government succeeded in arguing that the travel ban was necessary for national security. She said that no matter how much the government tried to "launder" Mr. Trump's statements, "all of the evidence points in one direction."

Justice Sotomayor accused her colleagues in the majority of "unquestioning acceptance" of the president's national security claims. Justice Ruth Bader Ginsburg joined Justice Sotomayor's dissent. Justice Sotomayor accused the court of inconsistency, noting that a stray remark from a state commissioner expressing hostility to religion was the basis of a ruling this month in favor of a Christian baker who refused to create a cake for a same-sex wedding.

"Those principles should apply equally here," she wrote. "In both instances, the question is whether a government actor exhibited tolerance and neutrality in reaching a decision that affects individuals' fundamental religious freedom."

In a second, milder dissent, Justice Stephen G. Breyer, joined by Justice Elena Kagan, questioned whether the Trump administration could be trusted to enforce what he called "the proclamation's elaborate system of exemptions and waivers."

Justice Kennedy agreed that Mr. Trump should be allowed to carry out the travel ban, but he emphasized the need for religious tolerance.

"The First Amendment prohibits the establishment of religion and promises the free exercise of religion," he wrote. "It is an urgent necessity that officials adhere to these constitutional guarantees and mandates in all their actions, even in the sphere of foreign affairs. An anxious world must know that our government remains committed always to the liberties the Constitution seeks to preserve and protect, so that freedom extends outward, and lasts."

The court's decision, a major statement on presidential power, is the conclusion of a long-running dispute over Mr. Trump's authority to make good on his campaign promises to secure the United States' borders.

Only a week after he took office, Mr. Trump issued his first travel ban, causing chaos at the country's airports and starting a cascade of lawsuits and appeals. The first ban, drafted in haste, was promptly blocked by courts around the United States.

A second version, issued two months later, fared little better, although the Supreme Court allowed part of it go into effect last June when it agreed to hear the Trump administration's appeals from court decisions blocking it. But the Supreme Court dismissed those appeals in October after the second ban expired.

In January, the Supreme Court agreed to hear a challenge to Mr. Trump's third and most considered entry ban, the one issued as a presidential proclamation. It initially restricted travel from eight nations — Iran, Libya, Syria, Yemen, Somalia, Chad, Venezuela and North Korea — six of them predominantly Muslim. Chad was later removed from the list.

The restrictions varied in their details, but, for the most part, citizens of the countries were forbidden from emigrating to the United States, and many of them are barred from working, studying or vacationing here. In December, the Supreme Court allowed the ban to go into effect while legal challenges moved forward.

The State of Hawaii, several individuals and a Muslim group challenged the latest ban's limits on travel from the predominantly Muslim countries; they did not object to the portions concerning North Korea and Venezuela. They said the latest ban, like the earlier ones, was tainted by religious animus and not adequately justified by national security concerns.

The challengers prevailed before a Federal District Court in Hawaii and in San Francisco before a three-judge panel of the United States Court of Appeals for the Ninth Circuit.

The appeals court ruled that Mr. Trump had exceeded the authority Congress had given him over immigration and had violated a part of the immigration laws barring discrimination in the issuance of visas. In a separate decision that was not directly before the justices, the United States Court of Appeals for the Fourth Circuit, in Richmond, Va., blocked the ban on a different ground, saying it violated the Constitution's prohibition of religious discrimination.

TYLER BLINT-WELSH contributed reporting from New York.

Colorado Baker Sues Governor Over Cake Dispute With Transgender Woman

BY JULIE TURKEWITZ | AUG. 16, 2018

DENVER — The baker who won a United States Supreme Court case this year after refusing to make a cake for a same-sex wedding has sued the governor of Colorado, alleging the state discriminated against him when he declined to make a blue and pink cake for a transgender woman.

The lawsuit sets up yet another public battle involving Jack Phillips of Masterpiece Cakeshop over whether claims of religious freedoms can be used to refuse services to gay and transgender people. The Supreme Court did not definitively decide on that question in its ruling earlier this year, ensuring additional legal fights.

This time, the suit involves a customer, Autumn Scardina, who asked Mr. Phillips to make a cake with a blue exterior and pink interior that would mark her birthday and the seventh anniversary of her gender transition.

Mr. Phillips refused because the celebration ran contrary to his belief that gender is "given by God," his lawyers said, and "not determined by perceptions or feelings."

The suit, filed in Federal District Court in Denver this week, alleges that Colorado officials are on a "crusade" against Mr. Phillips because he refuses to make cakes that violate his religious beliefs. In recent years, his lawyers say, he has been targeted by potential customers eager to test the limit of the law.

On the same day in June 2017 that the Supreme Court agreed to hear the first case, the lawsuit says Ms. Scardina, a lawyer, called Masterpiece Cakeshop and requested the gender transition cake. Then, days after the Supreme Court ruling, the state's civil rights division issued

Jack Phillips, the owner of Masterpiece Cakeshop, at work in his store in Lakewood, Colo., in August 2017.

a decision finding probable cause that state law requires Mr. Phillips to make the new cake.

Mr. Phillips alleges that the state's decision violates his First Amendment rights to freely exercise his religious beliefs.

"The woman on the phone did not object to my request for a birthday cake until I told her I was celebrating my transition," Ms. Scardina wrote in a complaint to the state, explaining her interaction with one of Mr. Phillips's employees. "I was stunned."

Mr. Phillips's small bakery, with its cafe tables and glass case of cookies, is tucked into a shopping center in the Denver suburb of Lakewood. It became part of a national discussion over religious rights after Mr. Phillips received a 2012 visit from David Mullins and Charlie Craig, gay men looking for a wedding cake for a reception in Colorado.

Mr. Phillips declined, and the couple filed a complaint with the Colorado Civil Rights Commission, saying that Mr. Phillips had violated a state law barring discrimination based on sexual orientation. Mr. Mullins and Mr. Craig won before the state commission and in the state courts.

The U.S. Supreme Court ruled in Mr. Phillips's favor, but in doing so passed on the opportunity to rule on whether a business can refuse service to gay or transgender people by invoking First Amendment rights. Instead, in the majority opinion, Justice Anthony M. Kennedy argued that the Colorado Civil Rights Commission had been shown to be hostile to religion in that particular case.

"The outcome of cases like this in other circumstances must await further elaboration in the courts," he wrote.

Disputes concerning businesses that sell wedding services, including florists, calligraphers, photographers and videographers, are being litigated around the nation. Earlier this month, Justice Ruth Bader Ginsburg predicted that the question of whether there can be religious exemptions to anti-discrimination laws might soon return to the Supreme Court.

In an interview with Colorado Public Radio this week, Gov. John Hickenlooper, a Democrat, said that he supports religious freedom but does not believe Americans should be able to use it to deny service. "I don't think there should be bias involved of who you chose to serve and who you don't," he said.

But Mr. Phillips's lawyers, who are affiliated with the conservative Christian organization Alliance Defending Freedom, allege that the state of Colorado "is ignoring the message of the U.S. Supreme Court."

"Jack shouldn't have to fear government hostility when he opens his shop for business each day," they said in a statement. "We're asking the court to put a stop to that."

ADAM LIPTAK contributed reporting.

The Latest Attack on Islam: It's Not a Religion

OPINION | BY ASMA T. UDDIN | SEPT. 26, 2018

Too many Americans would deny Muslims the religious liberty they insist upon for Christians.

RELIGIOUS LIBERTY HAS become a particularly politicized topic in recent years, and recent months were no different. In a long-awaited June decision, the Supreme Court decided in favor of a Christian baker who refused to make a custom wedding cake for a gay couple. In July, Attorney General Jeff Sessions introduced a "religious liberty task force" that critics saw as a mere cover for anti-gay discrimination. And Judge Brett Kavanaugh's record has been scoured for evidence of what his appointment to the Supreme Court would mean for future decisions in which Christian beliefs clash with law and policy.

But when it comes to religious liberty for Americans, there's a disturbing trend that has drawn much less attention. In recent years, state lawmakers, lawyers and influential social commentators have been making the case that Muslims are not protected by the First Amendment.

Why? Because, they argue, Islam is not a religion.

This once seemed like an absurd fringe argument. But it has gained momentum. John Bennett, a Republican state legislator in Oklahoma, said in 2014, "Islam is not even a religion; it is a political system that uses a deity to advance its agenda of global conquest." In 2015, a former assistant United States attorney, Andrew C. McCarthy, wrote in National Review that Islam "should be understood as conveying a belief system that is not merely, or even primarily, religious." In 2016, Michael Flynn, who the next year was briefly President Trump's national security adviser, told an ACT for America conference in Dallas that "Islam is a political ideology" that "hides behind the notion of it being a religion." In a January 2018 news release, Neal Tapio of South Dakota, a Republican state senator who was planning to run for the United States House of Representatives, questioned whether the First Amendment applies to Muslims.

The idea that Islam, which has over 1.6 billion adherents worldwide, is not a religion was even deployed in a 2010 legal challenge of county approval of building plans for a mosque in Murfreesboro, Tenn. The plaintiffs argued that Islam is not a religion but rather a geopolitical system bent on instituting jihadist and Shariah law in America. Because Islam is not a religion, the argument went, the mosque construction plans should not benefit from the county or federal laws that protect religious organizations. The local court ruled against the mosque, but the Tennessee appellate court overturned the ruling and the mosque prevailed.

This argument about land use is particularly distressing because not too long ago, a bipartisan coalition in Congress helped enact the federal Religious Land Use and Institutionalized Persons Act to prevent discriminatory or burdensome regulations from restricting religious exercise. In 2000, it passed both the House and the Senate by unanimous consent, as lawmakers expressed concern that minority faiths disproportionately faced zoning conflicts, and was signed into law by President Bill Clinton. It's jarring that some would now argue that these protections do not apply to Muslims.

At the root of the push to deny that Islam is a religion is a misguided belief that Muslims are anti-American. An industry of anti-Muslim fearmongering has helped stoke and perpetuate moral panic about Islam taking over America and subverting American values.

A 2016 survey by the Pew Research Center found that almost half of all American adults believed that "at least some" American Muslims are anti-American; this number included 11 percent who think "most" or "almost all" American Muslims are anti-American. Fourteen percent thought that about half of all American Muslims are against America. A 2017 poll found that half of United States adults

A mosque in Washington. In recent years, state lawmakers and others have been arguing that Muslims are not protected by the First Amendment.

believed that Islam does not have a place in "mainstream American society," and almost half (44 percent) thought there was a "natural conflict between Islam and democracy." The fear is so real that in 2010, when the mosque opponents in Murfreesboro argued against the religious validity of Islam, the Department of Justice filed an amicus brief explaining that "under the United States Constitution and other federal laws, it is uncontroverted that Islam is a religion, and a mosque is a place of religious assembly."

The fear is not limited to mosque cases. There have been legislative efforts in 43 states to ban the practice of Islamic religious law, or Shariah law; 24 bills were introduced in 2017 alone, according to the Haas Institute at the University of California, Berkeley. This year, Idaho introduced an anti-Shariah bill, bringing the number of measures introduced since 2010 to at least 217. Of those, 20 have been enacted.

The laws' backers seem to see them as necessary stopgaps to protect against their imagined Muslim takeover of America. When an Idaho state representative, Eric Redman, a Republican, introduced his anti-Shariah bill in January, he said it was needed so that "foreign law" would not "defile our constitutional laws" and to "protect our state and our country." That's a similar sentiment to the one expressed by the conservative political activist Pamela Geller, who argued in a 2016 commentary published by Breitbart that Muslim women seeking accommodations to wear a head scarf in the workplace are part of a "Muslim effort to impose Islam on the secular marketplace."

It's not hard to imagine what the reaction from these corners would be if Muslims sought other exemptions, including ones routinely sought by Christians — from performing certain medical procedures, providing certain medications or, say, from baking a wedding cake for a gay couple. A June poll by Morning Consult showed that white evangelicals are more likely to support religious business owners refusing services to L.G.B.T. individuals if the business owner is a Christian, Jew or Mormon — but less so if the business owner is a Muslim.

If Islamophobes are successful in their efforts to strip American Muslims of the same protections that Christians enjoy, it's they — not the Muslims they irrationally fear — who will be responsible for curtailing religious liberty.

ASMA T. UDDIN, a religious liberty lawyer and scholar, is the author of the forthcoming book "When Islam Is Not a Religion."

Glossary

arbitrary Based on a random choice instead of on a system or reason.

blue laws The prohibition of activities such as shopping on a Sunday.

Catholic A member of the Roman Catholic Church.

common law English laws that have been changed and adopted to different US states and the federal government.

concubinage Keeping a concubine, or a woman who lives with a man but does not have the status of a wife.

connexion Another form of the word "connection."

conscientious objector A person who objects to serving in the U.S. military due to their conscience.

denomination An independent, recognized branch of Christianity.

desecrate Treating a sacred thing or place with extreme disrespect.

dogma A set of religious beliefs that church authorities proclaim is true.

ecclesiastical Relating to the Christian clergy or church.

encyclical A letter sent by the Pope to the bishops of the Catholic church.

evangelical According to teachings of Christianity.

Orthodox Hebrew A branch of traditional Judaism.

ostensibly The appearance of truth.

parochial Relating to a church's parish.

plural marriage When a man has more than one wife.

polygamy When a man marries more than one woman.

poorhouse An institution that cares for the poor at the public expense.

Protestant A member of Christian churches that have separated from the Roman Catholic Church.

Rabbi A teacher or scholar in the Jewish faith.

Romanism Another word for Roman Catholicism.

Sabbath A day of the week free from work and set aside for religious services.

sacrilege Disrespect toward something sacred.

transgender A person who identifies as a gender different from the one they were assigned at birth.

Vatican A city-state in Rome that is the seat of the Pope and the Roman Catholic Church.

Media Literacy Terms

"Media literacy" refers to the ability to access, understand, critically assess and create media. The following terms are important components of media literacy, and they will help you critically engage with the articles in this title.

angle The aspect of a news story that a journalist focuses on and develops.

attribution The method by which a source is identified or by which facts and information are assigned to the person who provided them.

balance Principle of journalism that both perspectives of an argument should be presented in a fair way.

chronological order Method of writing a story presenting the details of the story in the order in which they occurred.

column A type of story that is a regular feature, often on a recurring topic, written by the same journalist, generally known as a columnist.

commentary A type of story that is an expression of opinion on recent events by a journalist generally known as a commentator.

credibility The quality of being trustworthy and believable, said of a journalistic source.

critical review A type of story that describes an event or work of art, such as a theater performance, film, concert, book, restaurant, radio or television program, exhibition or musical piece, and offers critical assessment of its quality and reception.

editorial Article of opinion or interpretation.

feature story Article designed to entertain as well as to inform.

human interest story A type of story that focuses on individuals and how events or issues affect their life, generally offering a sense of relatability to the reader.

impartiality Principle of journalism that a story should not reflect a journalist's bias and should contain balance.

intention The motive or reason behind something, such as the publication of a news story.

interview story A type of story in which the facts are gathered primarily by interviewing another person or persons.

motive The reason behind something, such as the publication of a news story or a source's perspective on an issue.

news story An article or style of expository writing that reports news, generally in a straightforward fashion and without editorial comment.

op-ed An opinion piece that reflects a prominent individual's opinion on a topic of interest.

paraphrase The summary of an individual's words, with attribution, rather than a direct quotation of their exact words.

reliability The quality of being dependable and accurate, said of a journalistic source.

rhetorical device Technique in writing intending to persuade the reader or communicate a message from a certain perspective.

source The origin of the information reported in journalism.

style A distinctive use of language in writing or speech; also a news or publishing organization's rules for consistent use of language with regard to spelling, punctuation, typography and capitalization, usually regimented by a house style guide.

tone A manner of expression in writing or speech.

Media Literacy Questions

1. "A Blow at Polygamy" (on page 46), provides paraphrased information from George Reynolds. What are the strengths of the use of a paraphrase as opposed to a direct quote? What are the weaknesses?

2. Compare the headlines of "Sabbath a Day of Rest" (on page 55) and "Senate on Sunday Laws" (on page 64). Which is a more compelling headline, and why? How could the less compelling headline be changed to better draw the reader's interest?

3. Does Lewis Wood demonstrate the journalistic principle of impartiality in his article "High Court Backs State Right to Run Parochial Buses" (on page 136)? If so, how did he do so? If not, what could he have included to make the article more impartial?

4. The article "The Latest Attack on Islam: It's Not a Religion" (on page 207) is an example of an op-ed. Identify how Asma T. Uddin's attitude and tone help convey her opinion on the topic.

5. Does "Religious Liberty Found Advancing" (on page 134) use multiple sources? What are the strengths of using multiple sources in a journalistic piece? What are the weaknesses of relying heavily on only one or a few sources?

6. "Excerpts From Decision on Separation of Church and State" (on page 144) compares two viewpoints. What are the similarities between the two viewpoints? What are the differences?

7. Analyze the authors' reporting in "Religious Liberty in Alaskan Islands" (on page 104) and "Use of Drugs in Religious Rituals Can Be Prosecuted, Justices Rule" (on page 161). Do you think one journalist is more balanced in their reporting than the other? If so, why do you think so?

8. Often, as a news story develops, a journalist's attitude toward the subject may change. Compare "Boston Archdiocese Asks for Dismissal of All Suits" (on page 181) and "In Narrow Decision, Supreme Court Sides With Baker Who Turned Away Gay Couple" (on page 191), both by Adam Liptak. Did new information discovered between the publication of these two articles change Liptak's perspective on social issues?

9. "High Court Rules Religious Clubs Can Meet in Public High Schools" (on page 164) and "The White House Puts the Bible Before the Hippocratic Oath" (on page 184) are examples of two different journalistic styles. How do they differ from one another in the information they present? What techniques do they use to convey that information?

10. Identify each of the sources in "Arab Girls' Veils at Issue in France" (on page 149) as a primary source or a secondary source. Evaluate the reliability and credibility of each source. How does your evaluation of each source change your perspective on this article?

11. "Trump's Travel Ban Is Upheld by Supreme Court" (on page 197) is a joint effort between journalists Adam Liptak and Michael D. Shear. Does this article differ in style and tone from "In Order, President Eases Limits on U.S. Aid to Religious Groups" (on page 177) by a single journalist, Richard W. Stevenson? What elements helped you come to your conclusion?

Citations

All citations in this list are formatted according to the Modern Language Association's (MLA) style guide.

BOOK CITATION

THE NEW YORK TIMES EDITORIAL STAFF. *Religious Freedom.* New York: New York Times Educational Publishing, 2020.

ONLINE ARTICLE CITATIONS

BERGER, JOSEPH. "New York Church Leaders Divided Over Homosexual-Rights Measures." *The New York Times*, 9 Feb. 1986, timesmachine .nytimes.com/timesmachine/1986/02/09/725586.html.

EGAN, TIMOTHY. "Anti-Abortion Bill in Idaho Takes Aim At Landmark Case." *The New York Times*, 22 Mar. 1990, www.nytimes.com/1990/03/22/us/anti -abortion-bill-in-idaho-takes-aim-at-landmark-case.html.

GETTLEMAN, JEFFREY. "Judge's Biblical Monument Is Ruled Unconstitutional." *The New York Times*, 19 Nov. 2002, timesmachine.nytimes.com /timesmachine/2002/11/19/984558.html.

GOODSTEIN, LAURIE. "Voucher Ruling Seen as Further Narrowing Church-State Division." *The New York Times*, 28 June 2002, https://timesmachine .nytimes.com/timesmachine/2002/06/28/759040.html.

GREENHOUSE, LINDA. "High Court Rules Religious Clubs Can Meet in Public High Schools." *The New York Times*, 5 June 1990, timesmachine.nytimes .com/timesmachine/1990/06/05/987390.html.

GREENHOUSE, LINDA. "Use of Drugs in Religious Rituals Can Be Prosecuted, Justices Rule." *The New York Times*, 18 Apr. 1990, www.nytimes.com/1990/04/18 /us/use-of-drugs-in-religious-rituals-can-be-prosecuted-justices-rule.html.

IBRAHIM, YOUSSEF M. "Arab Girls' Veils At Issue In France." *The New York Times*, 12 Nov. 1989, www.nytimes.com/1989/11/12/world/arab-girls-veils-at -issue-in-france.html.

KOHLER, MAX J. "Religious Liberty in Alaskan Islands." *The New York Times*, 10 Sept. 1905, timesmachine.nytimes.com/timesmachine/1905/09/10/101330601.html.

LAMBERT, BRUCE. "A Church-State Conflict Arises Over AIDS Care." *The New York Times*, 23 Feb. 1990, timesmachine.nytimes.com/timesmachine/1990/02/23/445790.html.

LIPTAK, ADAM. "Boston Archdiocese Asks for Dismissal of All Suits." *The New York Times*, 24 Dec. 2002, www.nytimes.com/2002/12/24/us/boston-archdiocese-asks-for-dismissal-of-all-suits.html.

LIPTAK, ADAM. "In Narrow Decision, Supreme Court Sides With Baker Who Turned Away Gay Couple." *The New York Times*, 4 June 2018, www.nytimes.com/2018/06/04/us/politics/supreme-court-sides-with-baker-who-turned-away-gay-couple.html.

LIPTAK, ADAM, AND MICHAEL D. SHEAR. "Trump's Travel Ban Is Upheld by Supreme Court." *The New York Times*, 26 June 2018, www.nytimes.com/2018/06/26/us/politics/supreme-court-trump-travel-ban.html.

THE NEW YORK TIMES. "Against the Salvation Army." *The New York Times*, 29 July 1899, timesmachine.nytimes.com/timesmachine/1899/07/29/117928648.html.

THE NEW YORK TIMES. "Aiming at Religion." *The New York Times*, 12 Sept. 1881, timesmachine.nytimes.com/timesmachine/1881/09/12/102759559.html.

THE NEW YORK TIMES. "Austrian Progress — Religions Liberty — The Press Law in Hungary." *The New York Times*, 26 Mar. 1868, timesmachine.nytimes.com/timesmachine/1868/03/26/78911198.html.

THE NEW YORK TIMES. "A Blow at Polygamy." *The New York Times*, 8 Jan. 1879, timesmachine.nytimes.com/timesmachine/1879/01/08/80741662.html.

THE NEW YORK TIMES. "Church and State In Europe." *The New York Times*, 14 Dec. 1874, timesmachine.nytimes.com/timesmachine/1874/12/14/82746254.html.

THE NEW YORK TIMES. "Civil and Religious Liberty." *The New York Times*, 1 Feb. 1874, timesmachine.nytimes.com/timesmachine/1874/02/01/79215719.html.

THE NEW YORK TIMES. "Conscientious Objectors." *The New York Times*, 16 Feb. 1919, timesmachine.nytimes.com/timesmachine/1919/02/16/97074142.html.

THE NEW YORK TIMES. "Dr. Wise Against Repeal of Dry Law." *The New York Times*, 12 Apr. 1920, timesmachine.nytimes.com/timesmachine/1920/04/12/96882229.html.

THE NEW YORK TIMES. "To Enforce Sunday Laws." *The New York Times*, 2 Oct. 1920, timesmachine.nytimes.com/timesmachine/1920/10/02 /102898391.html.

THE NEW YORK TIMES. "Excerpts From Decision on Separation of Church and State." *The New York Times*, 30 June 1988, www.nytimes.com/1988/06/30 /us/the-supreme-court-excerpts-from-decision-on-separation-of-church -and-state.html.

THE NEW YORK TIMES. "The Freedom of Worship Bill." *The New York Times*, 16 Feb. 1885, timesmachine.nytimes.com/timesmachine/1885/02/16 /106299497.html.

THE NEW YORK TIMES. "A Fruit Of Civilization." *The New York Times*, 22 Nov. 1894, timesmachine.nytimes.com/timesmachine/1894/11/22/106880681 .html.

THE NEW YORK TIMES. " 'Healer' to Be Prosecuted." *The New York Times*, 31 Jan. 1901, timesmachine.nytimes.com/timesmachine/1901/01/31 /101068801.html.

THE NEW YORK TIMES. "Hearing at Albany for Christian Scientists." *The New York Times*, 31 Jan. 1901, timesmachine.nytimes.com/timesmachine/1901 /01/31/101068801.html.

THE NEW YORK TIMES. "High Court Voids Jehovah Sect Curb." *The New York Times*, 21 May 1940, timesmachine.nytimes.com/timesmachine/1940 /05/21/92979985.html.

THE NEW YORK TIMES. "Imprisonment of a Young Woman in New-York for Turning Protestant." *The New York Times*, 11 July 1868, timesmachine .nytimes.com/timesmachine/1868/07/11/78921496.html.

THE NEW YORK TIMES. "Lord Russell and Religious Liberty." *The New York Times*, 29 May 1878, timesmachine.nytimes.com/timesmachine/1878/05 /29/80684075.html.

THE NEW YORK TIMES. "New York City and the Ironclad Sunday Law." *The New York Times*, 8 Dec. 1907, timesmachine.nytimes.com/timesmachine /1907/12/08/104712644.html.

THE NEW YORK TIMES. "The Quakers on the Draft Further Views on the Subject." *The New York Times*, 27 Aug. 1864, timesmachine.nytimes.com /timesmachine/1864/08/27/80297738.html.

THE NEW YORK TIMES. "Quakers Pledge Aid to Nation in War." *The New York Times*, 29 May 1917, timesmachine.nytimes.com/timesmachine/1917/05 /29/102348484.html.

THE NEW YORK TIMES. "Religious Liberty Found Advancing." *The New York Times*, 3 July 1939, timesmachine.nytimes.com/timesmachine/1939/07/03/93936714.html.

THE NEW YORK TIMES. "Religious Liberty in the United States." *The New York Times*, 23 Apr. 1876, https://timesmachine.nytimes.com/timesmachine/1876/04/23/80625894.html.

THE NEW YORK TIMES. "Religious Persecution to Cease." *The New York Times*, 8 Nov. 1895, timesmachine.nytimes.com/timesmachine/1895/11/08/102480284.html.

THE NEW YORK TIMES. "Religious Toleration in Mexico — The Progress Made under Maximilian." *The New York Times*, 21 Nov. 1866, timesmachine.nytimes.com/timesmachine/1866/11/21/83464343.html.

THE NEW YORK TIMES. "Sabbath a Day of Rest." *The New York Times*, 27 Dec. 1896, timesmachine.nytimes.com/timesmachine/1896/12/27/108271289.html.

THE NEW YORK TIMES. "Senate on Sunday Laws." *The New York Times*, 1 Feb. 1899, timesmachine.nytimes.com/timesmachine/1899/02/01/117911938.html.

THE NEW YORK TIMES. "Shall We Have a Sabbath ?" *The New York Times*, 17 Oct. 1867, timesmachine.nytimes.com/timesmachine/1867/10/17/79355353.html.

THE NEW YORK TIMES. "Sunday Closing Campaign." *The New York Times*, 13 Feb. 1899, timesmachine.nytimes.com/timesmachine/1899/02/13/118934154.html.

THE NEW YORK TIMES. "Sunday Under the Penal Code." *The New York Times*, 3 Dec. 1882, timesmachine.nytimes.com/timesmachine/1882/12/03/102934276.html.

THE NEW YORK TIMES. "The Utah Constitution." *The New York Times*, 20 May 1895, timesmachine.nytimes.com/timesmachine/1895/05/20/106062472.html.

THE NEW YORK TIMES. "The War Upon Polygamy." *The New York Times*, 7 Oct. 1886, timesmachine.nytimes.com/timesmachine/1886/10/07/103987177.html.

THE NEW YORK TIMES. "The White House Puts the Bible Before the Hippocratic Oath." *The New York Times*, 29 Jan. 2018, www.nytimes.com/2018/01/28/opinion/editorials/white-house-religious-freedom-doctors.html.

STEVENSON, RICHARD W. "In Order, President Eases Limits on U.S. Aid to Religious Groups." *The New York Times*, 13 Dec. 2002, www.nytimes.com /2002/12/13/us/in-order-president-eases-limits-on-us-aid-to-religious -groups.html.

TURKEWITZ, JULIE. "Colorado Baker Sues Governor Over Cake Dispute With Transgender Woman." *The New York Times*, 16 Aug. 2018, www.nytimes .com/2018/08/16/us/masterpiece-cakeshop-colorado-jack-phillips.html.

UDDIN, ASMA T. "The Latest Attack on Islam: It's Not a Religion." *The New York Times*, 26 Sept. 2018, www.nytimes.com/2018/09/26/opinion /islamophobia-muslim-religion-politics.html.

UDDIN, ASMA. "What Islamophobic Politicians Can Learn From Mormons." *The New York Times*, 22 May 2018, www.nytimes.com/2018/05/22/opinion /mormons-islamophobia-utah.html.

WOOD, LEWIS. "High Court Backs State Right to Run Parochial Buses." *The New York Times*, 11 Feb. 1947, timesmachine.nytimes.com /timesmachine/1947/02/11/93788941.html.

WOOD, LEWIS. "Supreme Court Ends Compulsion of Flag Salute." *The New York Times*, 15 June 1943, timesmachine.nytimes.com/timesmachine /1943/06/15/85106963.html.

Index

This book is current up until the time of printing. For the most up-to-date reporting, visit www.nytimes.com.